My Daily Journey with
My Utmost for His Highest

Discovery
House
PUBLISHERS

BOX 3566 · GRAND RAPIDS, MI 49501

*PUBLISHING BOOKS THAT FEED
THE SOUL WITH THE WORD OF GOD.*

My
Daily
Journey
with
My Utmost
for
His Highest

Personal Reflections
That Draw Us
Closer to God

Carolyn Reeves

Dedication

To Bernice,
who gave me my first copy of *My Utmost for His Highest,*
and to my daughters, Ashley and Kimberly,
who gave me the freedom to pour over it for many hours.

My Daily Journey with My Utmost for His Highest
Copyright © 1995 Carolyn Reeves

Discovery House Publishers is affiliated with RBC Ministries, Grand Rapids, Michigan 49512.

Discovery House books are distributed to the trade by Thomas Nelson Publishers, Nashville, Tennessee 37214.

Library of Congress Cataloging-in-Publication Data

Reeves, Carolyn.
 My daily journey with my utmost for His highest : personal reflections that draw us closer to God / by Carolyn Reeves.
 p. cm.

 ISBN 1-57293-005-5

 1. Devotional calendars. 2. Spiritual exercises. 3. Chambers, Oswald, 1874–1917. My Utmost for His Highest. I. Title.
BV4811.C4553R44 1995
242'.2–dc20   95-33978
                           CIP

Printed in the United States of America

95 96 97 98 99 00 / CHG / 10 9 8 7 6 5 4 3 2 1

Foreword

Next to the Bible, *My Utmost for His Highest* is my favorite book. I believe it gives sound counsel for every Christian. The purpose of this journaling workbook is to help you with your spiritual progress. Faithful study, prayer, and journaling will enable you to see life from God's point of view.

January 1

1. What keeps me from being my utmost for His highest?

2. An area where I am reluctant to yield to Jesus is

3. What can I do today to be my utmost?

4. Choose the statement(s) that best apply. I am hindered by
   ❏ too much consideration for myself.
   ❏ pretending to consider others.
   ❏ what it will cost others.

5. I will keep myself before God by

6. The crisis causing me to choose for or against God is

January 2

1. What prevents my daily going out and placing my confidence in God?

2. An instance when I wasted time and energy by worrying needlessly was

3. When I ask God what He is going to do, He reveals instead who He is because

4. I believe (or refuse to believe) in a miracle-working God because

5. I am learning to go out trusting in God in the area of

January 3

1. How does knowing who Jesus is, as contrasted with what He does, make such a difference in my life?

2. Is there an area in my life where I am experiencing clouds and darkness about who Jesus is? What is it?

3. As I wait on God and meditate on His Word, these clouds and darkness become

January 4

1. Is there something I want to do, but find it hard to understand why I can't do it now?

2. Why would it be a mistake to fill that need on my own without waiting for God to bring it about?

3. How do I know when God is not guiding?

4. Is there an area in my life where my allegiance to God may be natural devotion?

5. What key insight have I gained about my loyalty to God?

JANUARY 5

1. How do I move from external devotion to Jesus to an internal martyrdom for Jesus?

2. Do I find a sense of peace in the awareness that I cannot do this myself?

3. How will I come to the end of myself?

JANUARY 6

1. When I receive a spiritual blessing from God, why must I give it back to Him?

2. When a vessel develops dry rot, does it lose its value?

3. Will I always know when a blessing I have given back to God is being used by Him?

4. Why is my public activity for God dependent upon my private communion with Him?

5. What am I learning about worship, waiting, and work?

JANUARY 7

1. The reason Jesus is the last one with whom I become intimate is

2. Why is friendship so rare?

3. What is the purpose of the discipline of life?

4. Do I desire to know Jesus in a deeper way? Why?

5. Some advantages of knowing Christ well are

JANUARY 8

1. The differences between a one-time physical death for God, and the sacrifice in Romans 12:1 are

2. The bands that may be hindering my spiritual walk with Jesus are

3. These bands are loosened by

JANUARY 9

1. What is involved in walking in the light?

2. How do I become estranged from God's light?

3. Is there an area in my life where I am tempted to keep God's light from shining?

4. How does staying open and honest in God's presence help?

JANUARY 10

1. Why do I sometimes fail in my personal Christian experience?

2. I think the difference between conversion and salvation is

3. I know I am born again because

4. I know this because of my own decision to

5. When I am sanctified, I give up my right to

JANUARY 11

1. The last time others' plans were upset because I obeyed God, the result for them and God and me was

2. I handled their reactions by

3. I was tempted to prevent their suffering because

4. I believe the sting is (or is not) inevitable because

5. If I obey God, what will He do for those who were caught up in the results of my obedience?

JANUARY 12

1. What do I discover about myself as God takes me on a journey through the nooks and crannies of my own life?

2. What wrong response to a crisis have I found myself repeating?

3. What do I think as I reflect on the incident?

4. What is the opposite response to making excuses for my character weaknesses?

5. What is the last conceit to go?

6. God is dealing with me over the issue of

JANUARY 13

1. What has God taught me through negative circumstances?

2. Why were the people outside my circumstances not perplexed?

3. Read John 14:26. What terms are used to describe the Holy Spirit? What does the verse say He will do?

4. Am I aware of how God deals with my soul? Explain.

5. Why does God teach compassion for others?

6. How will I get beyond all my questioning?

JANUARY 14

1. When it comes to God's call, my ears are

2. My attitude about going is

3. I am (or am not) willing to prove myself a chosen one by

4. If I pursue God, and the Spirit of God brings me face-to-face with God, then I will

January 15

1. Why is a white funeral necessary?

2. My white funeral experience, or the closest I've come to it in my life, was when

3. Once I have had this experience, and my only purpose is to be a witness for Him, nothing can defeat me because

4. Has God placed me in circumstances that help me stop striving? Explain.

5. Because I feel ready to go through with my white funeral experience now, I will write a prayer telling God.

January 16

1. How do I hear the call of God?

2. Which of God's attributes causes Him to call me to be used?

3. A strand of God's call at work in me is

4. What prevents me from hearing the call of God?

5. Am I willing to be altered so that I am able to hear God's call?

JANUARY 17

1. Match and then put in order of occurrence in my life.

   Two ways I am serving God out of my love for Him are

   ___ Service
   ___ I realize what I desire to do
       for Him
   ___ God's call

   b. when I come into contact
       with His nature.
   c. is expressive of God's nature.
   a. is fitted to my own nature.

2. One way I feel He is preparing me to serve Him in the future is

JANUARY 18

1. I want to be broken bread and poured out wine for my Lord now because

2. I will be devoted to the Lord Jesus if I

3. One way I plan to satisfy Jesus today is by

4. I can be poured out completely rather than just serve my Lord if I will

5. The best way I can be used by God in His battles is to

JANUARY 19

1. The vision I have just now is

2. I cannot see exactly what God wants to do, therefore I will

3. God is dealing with my self-sufficiency or presumption by

4. God is more real to me now than ever before because

JANUARY 20

1. In what way is my life like this description?

   Because I am born again from above, my life is always like a new beginning, full of freshness and surprise.

2. Do I feel fresh at this very moment or stale, frantically searching my mind for something to do? Explain.

3. Is there some area I have closed off to God? If so, explain.

4. Am I willing to open this area to Jesus Christ? I will not merely pretend to be open because

JANUARY 21

1. One area where I am kind to God is

2. One area in my life where I want to begin blessing the heart of God is

3. The thing in my life that hinders me from being full of extravagant love for my Savior is that
   - ❏ I like money and things more just now.
   - ❏ I want to please someone else more.
   - ❏ I feel insecure about a relationship.
   - ❏ I don't want to give up something.
   - ❏ I value my time for work or leisure.
   - ❏ I want to please myself.
   - ❏ I

4. With eternity in mind, I will write a brief prayer to God about my priorities.

JANUARY 22

1. Am I looking to God, or am I looking at what I want from God?

2. Do my expectations of Him hinder my ability to know Him? How?

3. What problems are keeping me from concentrating on God?

4. What blessings are fracturing my focus on God?

January 23

1. Is there some good thing hindering me from the very best God has for me? What is it?

2. Is it hard to keep my focus "above"? How can I learn this discipline?

3. The things in my life that obscure my concentration on God are

4. I often want to attain an image in this world that relates to a passing fad. While this may be OK, it is not God's highest. Am I willing to go for the best image? I will make an effort today by

January 24

1. Am I ready to be overpowered by the Lord?

2. Here is a brief statement about how I am doing in the following areas:

   My whole life is overpowered by the Lord, and aside from Him I have

   no end –
   no aim –
   no purpose –

3. Is knowing the Master and His will a continual revelation to me?

4. Once I have a vision of what He wants me to do, why should I stay connected?

5. Do I need to be mastered (overpowered) on a continual basis? How can I do that and why should I?

JANUARY 25

1. Describe a time when I prayed expecting God to answer in a certain way.

2. Explain how He did (or did not) answer in the way I expected Him to (Ephesians 3:20).

3. Because God sees the bigger picture I can

JANUARY 26

1. When was the last time I lost communion with Jesus because of some earthly care?

2. Why is it difficult to be simple like a child and trust my heavenly Father?

3. My pride, lust, or impatience hinders me here. Which is most common with me?

4. How do I keep my feathers from being ruffled or singed by the world?

1. Do I find it disconcerting that I am never free of the constant temptation to be overly preoccupied with cares?

2. Is it the disturbance of my "comfort zone" or the way I look to others that causes me to fret?

3. Is there a thought about my life that is in competition with my relatedness to Jesus right now?

JANUARY 28

1. What is the truth about my rights and my dignity?

2. How does exercising my stubborn will hurt Jesus?

3. One situation or circumstance where I rely on self-respect is

   How does this grieve His Spirit?

4. Is God meek? Explain.

5. What would happen if God answered every prayer as I wanted Him to?

6. Am I willing to prevent the persecution of Jesus? How will I do this?

January 29

1. What is God saying to me in my circumstances?

2. Am I passing the test, or must I keep repeating it?

3. Is there a way I am hurting Jesus? If so, how?

4. What will I do to stop hurting Jesus?

5. What should be my greatest aim?

January 30

1. Why doesn't God make Himself perfectly clear when He speaks to me?

2. What am I discerning that God is saying in my circumstances now?

3. Am I trying to prevent suffering in the life of another person where God is concerned?

4. At what cost will I do this?

5. Why do I ask others when God wants me to decide?

JANUARY 31

1. Have I gotten beyond concentrating on my own goodness?

2. What is the reality of redemption in terms of my own holiness or of anyone else's?

3. How do I feel about coming into contact with the rugged reality of redemption on behalf of the filth of human life, just as it is?

4. What will I do to begin my walk in reckless abandon to God?

FEBRUARY 1

1. Am I being egocentric about Jesus' redemption?

2. Do I feel insecure about my personal salvation and sanctification?

3. Where do these insecurities in me stem from?

4. To touch the underlying foundation of the gospel means

5. Today, my first step toward being more devoted to the gospel of God for the whole of humankind is to

February 2

1. If I choose to be a disciple of Jesus, what other conscious decisions must I make?

2. Why is it important to be reminded that I made this choice?

3. As I read through this list of ways I will need to die to myself, one area of competition that stands out in my life is

February 3

1. The last time I felt like refuse for the cause of Christ was when

2. When it came to finishing up the suffering of Christ, in being associated with Him, was I willing to be looked down on for Him?

3. Am I turned off by sinners, or do I see their need for a savior?

3. My last encounter with a sinner revealed my feelings of

February 4

1. Do I really believe that everything that happens in life reflects my response to God the Father and the cause of Christ?

2. What is one area where I realize that I am held in the viewpoint of God, or gripped by His love?

3. How do I prevent drawing attention to my own personal holiness?

February 5

Abased may be defined as "humbled" or "degraded."

In Luke 14:11 Jesus tells me that if I exalt myself I will be humbled, but if I humble myself, I will be exalted.

1. Do I really believe that God would ask me to be a doormat? Am I willing?

2. Why must I be humbled before I am able to be exalted?

3. I know it would bless God's heart if I would humble myself in serving Him by

February 6

1. Was there a point in time when I submitted my will to God and gave Him permission to purify my heart's desires?

2. Did I take that moment seriously? Did God take me seriously?

3. Do I recognize self-pity in myself? Do I encourage it?

4. Have I noticed the destruction of affinities or attachments that were not in God's best interests for me?

February 7

1. Do I sometimes expect God to do my part?

2. Why must I do my part?

3. What does the fact that God uses commonplace people and things have to do with answers to prayers?

4. Why do I need to seek God rather than just get His answer?

5. What is it like to get hold of God?

6. Am I able to be firm with myself about seeing and doing the commonplace?

FEBRUARY 8

1. With regard to this intense narrowing of interests, what current activity might God ask me to lay down or to greatly modify?

2. Am I willing to have God alter the way I spend my time and resources so that I may be more like Christ?

3. Do I want to be a person who holds God's point of view?

4. Will I lose some relationships?

5. Will I gain other relationships?

FEBRUARY 9

1. Am I spiritually exhausted because others draw their spiritual life from me?

2. What can replenish me?

3. First Corinthians 13 convinces me that everything I do in life must be motivated by, and built on, a foundation of

4. Is this action an individual striving? Is it an invitation for God to flow through me? Is it both?

FEBRUARY 10

1. I recall seeing God's grandeur in nature. One thing I remember is

   Another is

2. One or two "idols" that I spend too much time on are

3. How do these idols take the energy and creativity out of my prayer life?

4. Is God imaginative? Can He attach my prayers to the person He chooses?

FEBRUARY 11

1. Of the eagle and the chicken, which would I rather imitate? Why?

2. Have I been using my imagination wrongly?

3. Some ways I might use my gift of imagination to glorify God are

4. I will practice walking in God's presence by

FEBRUARY 12

1. Am I afraid to have God speak directly to me? Why or why not?

2. Do I fear what God will ask of me, or that I will be inconvenienced?

3. Have I ever tried to misunderstand His commands and His Word to avoid the responsibility of obedience? How?

4. Am I willing to really examine my heart on this issue?

5. Will I take the action God wants when I do?

FEBRUARY 13

1. Have I developed a friendship with God? How do I know His heart?

2. How will I get past this disrespect of mine and become aware of His speaking?

3. Am I so devoted to things, service, or convictions that I do not hear God? What specifically hinders me from hearing?

FEBRUARY 14

1. Am I going through a time of darkness about what God is doing in my life?

2. Why is it important to wait for greater understanding?

3. Why is it unprofitable to discuss with others where I am?

4. Do I recall a previous time when I came through a time of darkness and into this mixture of delight and humiliation?

5. What did I learn?

FEBRUARY 15

1. How will I respond now that I know I am responsible to God for the souls of people in my crowd?

2. Realizing that slackness in my relationship with God will cause others to suffer motivates me to

3. In which of these areas do I need the most improvement? Why?
   - ❏ physical selfishness
   - ❏ mental slovenliness
   - ❏ moral obtuseness
   - ❏ spiritual density

4. If I want to be a witness, why does it take time? Why must I be patient with myself?

FEBRUARY 16

1. When I was younger, did I believe I could change things in this world?

2. Why did I need to wait for the inspiration of God?

3. What do I learn while I am waiting?

4. I know I can make a difference in the world, but my thinking is different than youthful idealism. How does the inspiration of God make this difference?

FEBRUARY 17

1. What do I believe about the role depression plays in my life?

2. When I am depressed, what do I do, what should I do, and what will I do about my emotions?

3. Depression focuses on

   Doing the ordinary commonplace things focuses on

4. Is waiting for the Holy Spirit taking the initiative?

   Why does the Holy Spirit make the difference?

FEBRUARY 18

1. When have I experienced the hopeless despair of a lost opportunity that I needed to let sleep on the bosom of Christ?

2. Will I experience it again?

3. How can I "arise and do the next thing"?

4. What is the next thing for me?

5. Have I moved on with Jesus, my Lord?

6. Do I believe that my God is a God of new beginnings, fresh starts, and new actions?

FEBRUARY 19

1. What inescapable duties are drudgery to me?

2. Will it help to pray about these?

3. What does my response to drudgery have to do with my being spiritually "real"?

4. Have I been through drudgery with the inspiration of God on it? What was the task, and what was the result?

5. Has my view of menial tasks been changed because I observed another saint doing a menial task? What made the change?

6. Our drudgery is transfigured because

February 20

1. I am apt to dream about how to do a good job, but do I dream when I need to be about a responsibility God has given me?

One experience was

2. When is it appropriate to dream or meditate?

3. Have I found God's heart on something by quietly meditating? Have I ever just kept meditating when I already knew what to do? Why?

4. The next time this happens I will

February 21

1. Can I recall a time when I was carried away in my love for Jesus? What did I do?

2. Did I realize the Lord was watching me?

3. What look do I imagine was on His face as He watched my act of love for Him?

4. How am I able to show my abandon to God in my circumstance today?

5. Am I still focused on pleasing the Lord, or am I beginning to abandon myself to Him?

FEBRUARY 22

1. Is Jesus my hero?

2. Am I concerned that He will look bad or not win in the end?

3. Can I recall a time recently when it seemed as if the things Jesus stands for are just elusive hopes? Describe what happened.

4. Did I get a grip on the certainty that God is not going to be defeated? How did I work it out?

5. What noble dream am I holding to?

   What will be the most difficult thing about its fulfillment?

FEBRUARY 23

1. Am I a minister? In what ways do I see myself as a minister?

2. Where does love for service spring from?

3. How will I avoid being crushed in my service ministry?

4. What was I like and how did I treat the Savior before I gave in to His love?

5. Does this cause me to want to pray for, love, and serve others to the end of their meanness?

6. I will commit to pray for

February 24

1. Do I identify myself with Jesus Christ's interests and purposes in others? Explain.

2. Jesus is interested in

   I am interested in

3. Where am I in this great test with Jesus?

4. Where do I need to lay my life down in this area?

5. I don't throw my life away by wasting it on

6. Being alone with God in an effort to develop a holy life may render me of no value to others because

February 25

1. How does it strike me to be a servant of all?

2. Do I struggle when I must do things that get neither thanks nor applause from people?

3. Is it enough for me to know that I bless the heart of God in private?

4. Number in order of priority.
   ___ economic security
   ___ comfort
   ___ entertainment
   ___ pleasing God

5. I will write a brief prayer to God about my intentions and desire to serve Him without reservation.

FEBRUARY 26

1. What do I believe in actuality about the high ideals of Jesus?

2. Do I believe He can meet my needs if I am "in a spot"?

3. Is it a fact that I would rather not be put to this test? Why?

4. Does it humble me to know that I may need to let Him provide for me if I abandon myself and He puts me to the test?

I will write a brief prayer to the Lord relating my personal misgivings about His wits (abilities).

FEBRUARY 27

1. Have I been hindering what God could do in the depths of my being because I fail to believe in His almightiness?

2. What supernatural touch do I need in the depths of my person?
   - ❑ joy
   - ❑ peace
   - ❑ love
   - ❑ forgiveness
   - ❑ fulfillment
   - ❑ other

3. The impoverishment in me is there because

February 28

1. Is it possible that I am out of intimate contact with God at this time? How do I know?

2. Have I taken the stance of a superior person?

3. Have I been operating out of my own discernment or religious understanding? Explain.

4. If I am out of line, how will I get back into alignment with His resurrection life?

5. The action I will take to help keep me walking in the light is

February 29

1. The area remaining in my old life that disturbs me is

2. This area makes me a disturbance to others because

3. I have (have not) cried out to the Lord about this? Explain.

4. Have I trusted my common sense? Why doesn't this work?

5. I will not limit the Lord, but I will

MARCH 1

1. My love for Jesus could be described as

   ❏ a love that touches the center of my person.
   ❏ being a part of my confession before others.
   ❏ involving everything I do.

2. One Scripture passage that really hurts me when I read it is the one that says

3. This particular word from God hurts because

4. Why is being hurt by Jesus a most exquisite pain?

5. What makes it such a personal type of hurt?

MARCH 2

1. Why do I learn so much from the patient questioning of the Lord?

2. The sensitive place in my life where the Lord zeros in is

3. Is there an area where I will not be deluded again because God and I have already gone through this trial before and overcome it together?

4. What are three ways I may know the Lord has touched this area with His question(s)?

5. Did these questions reveal the amount of love I have for Jesus?

6. How did the Lord reveal me to myself?

March 3

1. God's final goal for me is that I become

2. How will the evidence of this be shown through me?

3. At this point in my life I am to feed the Father's sheep by

4. How does sympathy in me for myself or for others cause me to blaspheme the love of God?

March 4

1. My focus on His glory will cost me in the following ways:

2. Will I ever struggle with what it will cost me to follow Jesus?

3. Do I count my life as dear to myself?

4. Is this a process, or am I born again into this sacrificial view?

5. The decisions in my life are based upon
   ❑ common sense or practicality.
   ❑ where I will be of most use.
   ❑ the leading of my "Guide."
   ❑ where I will be most prosperous.
   ❑ my opportunities to see and do the most sports or activities.

March 5

1. I will find joy in life by

2. To obtain the joy of fulfillment in my life I will

3. Jesus found joy in His life by

4. What keeps me hanging in there when I know my reward may not even be realized in this lifetime?

5. Why must I ignore the demands of service along lines not relating to the call God has placed on my life?

March 6

1. The last time I simply had to do my duty by putting one foot in front of the other was

2. I experienced God's grace by

3. The way I worked it out by hands-on experience was

4. I was not crushed by this because

5. To keep the eyes of my spirit open to the risen Christ means I will

March 7

1. How does the very foundation of my faith prevent my separation from God?

2. Explain a time when a trial I faced produced joy. Why did it result in joy?

3. Do I possess undaunted radiance?

4. How do I develop this quality?

5. Is this a quality or more of an attitude?

6. How do I learn to ride out the high tides of life with joy?

March 8

1. Is there an area in my life before God or other people where I claim to be something that is not supported by the facts? Explain.

2. As I consider relinquishing everything in order to be worthy before God I feel
   - ❑ angry.
   - ❑ naked.
   - ❑ resistant.
   - ❑ other

3. Is God big enough to handle my emotions and love me all the same?

4. Does He appreciate my desire to be like His Son?

5. The positive side of this crisis of relinquishing is that God will give me and He will make me

March 9

1. Am I, by nature, a risk taker?

2. Do I possess a willingness toward Jesus to take risks?

3. How will I have a venturing attitude without being impulsive?

4. How will I stay dependent on and devoted to Jesus?

5. Why is it important to the Lord that my service for Him comes out of relationship with Him?

6. What do I have to offer apart from my relationship to Him?

March 10

A *sacrament* is "a formal religious act; a channel of communication between the earthly world and a world of spirits."

1. A time when I had the opportunity of being a spiritual messenger was

2. Have I been through the fire of God so that my life is like one set apart for His purposes?

3. Why would I need to have a life crumpled into the purpose of God before my life became the message?

4. Why must the liberation be real in me first before my message can liberate other souls?

MARCH 11

1. Why is it all over with the vision God has given if I don't live out my belief by bringing God into practical issues in my everyday life?

2. What does this have to do with giving my utmost for God's highest?

3. If I get so practical that I forget about the vision I will miss

4. Waiting tests my

5. One of God's storms in my life could be described as

6. I can prevent being an empty pod by (list 4 important ways)

MARCH 12

1. Some motives I see surface when I determine to surrender myself to God are

2. What specific obsession or priority would keep me from hearing God's call?
   - ❏ family
   - ❏ comforts
   - ❏ vanity
   - ❏ security
   - ❏ other

3. What is Jesus' response to my self-interest?

4. I will write a brief prayer telling God I will respond to His call, asking Him to help me go beyond my normal commitment. I will thank God that He will care for those I hurt as I respond to His call.

MARCH 13

1. To be delivered out of self and into a complete relationship with God would mean

2. As the Holy Spirit has put me in touch with God's personality, I have learned that He is

3. I am called to proclaim

4. What is the realization of Him that makes me want to surrender my life to Him?

MARCH 14

1. The power that dominates me is (see Galatians 5:19–23)

2. My bondage began when I

3. Do I have self-hatred?

4. How will I break free from the power that dominates me?

5. Do I want to be free?

MARCH 15

1. Have I experienced this essential season of distance in my walk with Christ?

2. What value could there be in my learning that Jesus has a point of view I know nothing about?

3. How does Jesus' deep understanding of sin and sorrow keep me from being friends with Him?

4. Why am I uncomfortable about this?

5. While I go through this time of darkness I will remember

MARCH 16

1. How will I avoid the dread of later judgment?

2. To live in the white light of Christ means

3. How will I know that I have "missed the mark"?

4. Is there a way I have sinned, and sin itself has paid me back in full?

5. The inherent consequences of sin can only be altered by

6. I was walking in unconscious unreality when I

MARCH 17

1. My greatest ambition is

2. Do I have the desire to please God above all else?

3. How could wrong ambition result in my being out of the race (a "cast-away")?

4. Why is the ambition to win souls or to establish churches a lower goal than being accepted by Him?

5. As I take stock of this week, my life is

MARCH 18

1. One bodily habit of mine that will not hold up under God's light is

2. To rid myself of this I will
   ❏ get prayer for it.
   ❏ get help by
   ❏ be accountable to
   ❏ other

3. An area in my thinking where I resist God's authority is

4. The area where I claim my right to myself is

5. I will deal with this by

MARCH 19

1. Why is it a snare to believe that God will lead me to success?

2. Is God building my character in any of these areas? How?

3. Some areas of faith where I have been tried and I have walked through and did not faint are

4. I believe beyond any doubt that
   ❑ God is
   ❑ God's Word is
   ❑ heaven is
   ❑ Jesus is
   ❑ my needs are
   ❑ my life is

MARCH 20

1. With regard to knowing God's will, due to my friendship with Him I might say that on a scale of 1 to 10 I am a ___.

2. The last time I felt God "check" me on an issue was when

3. My response to His check was

4. To know that "I am God's will" makes me feel

5. My understanding of God so far is
   ❑ He is very quiet.
   ❑ He is there, but
   ❑ I am doubting His goodness because
   ❑ other

March 21

1. Have I made a conscious choice to be crucified with Christ?

2. What happened as I began to give up my right to myself?

3. Did I allow the Holy Spirit to impart the holiness of Jesus to me?

4. In what area do I notice a change?

5. Is it apparent that I signed the death warrant on the disposition of sin? Explain.

March 22

1. The secret of the burning heart is to

2. One way I will abide in Jesus is

3. One emotion I have that I must not follow to its conclusion is

4. One activity I will do to follow the vision God has given me in a spiritually emotional time is

March 23

1. An area of struggle I noticed in myself after spiritual rebirth was

2. As I am exposed to God's Word the area I take exception to is

3. From now on I will respond to God by

4. A time when I proved my carnality was

5. I passed the test of resentment when I

March 24

1. If my sympathy gets in the way and says that some travesty does not belong in the life of another, how does this reflect on the Bridegroom?

2. The last time I sympathized with someone in the wrong thing, did I help him or her grow in God? Explain why not.

3. A time when I rejoiced in a right thing was when

4. I will help the Lord increase in the life of another by

I will decrease by

5. If I play the part of a rescuer, how do I hinder what God is trying to do in the life of another?

March 25

1. I will avoid leading others into wrong avenues, if they are attracted to my godliness, by

2. A time when I responded pridefully or wrongly was

3. Do I truly want Jesus to increase? Explain why.

   Am I willing to decrease? Explain how.

4. I will write a brief prayer about my willingness to decrease.

5. I will guard my relationship with the Bridegroom by

March 26

1. My purity suffers and I get out of harmony with God when I

2. When I become spotted and stained in my outer life I deal with it by

3. Because I want spiritual vision from God I will

4. Recently I have been tarnished by

5. Because I want intimacy with God, some activities I plan to avoid are

MARCH 27

1. How much do I long to go up higher with my God?

2. When I am exposed to new spiritual knowledge, will it be accompanied with temptation or grace, or both?

Here's an example from my life today.

3. Does temptation have any value? What value?

4. The kinds of transactions that take place in heavenly places to which God takes me are

MARCH 28

1. A directive God is giving me now may be

2. I know the opportunity to obey Him comes from Him because

3. A time when I was obedient and God received honor was

4. The difference in operating on faith rather than on intellect is

5. Why obey with reckless or unrestrained joy?

March 29

1. The reason I don't face Jesus at every turn is

2. At this time I am absorbed in

3. I sincerely believe that

   ❏ I have the desire to face Jesus.
   ❏ I have the desire to be spiritually real.
   ❏ I want to expect Him at every turn.
   ❏ I want to be filled with childlike wonder.

4. Because I want to do these things I will

   ❏ give up being religious (with His help).
   ❏ be willing to be considered impractical or a daydreamer.
   ❏ trust no one who blocks my facing Him.

March 30

To *intercede* means "to plead for another." To *worship* means "to take part in prayer, service, show intense love or reverence for."

1. How do my statements of unbelief betray my attitude toward worship?

2. What does my relationship to God have to do with my worship of Him?

3. If I am hard or dogmatic, how do I find my proper relationship to God again?

4. Intercessory prayer has no hidden pitfalls because

MARCH 31

1. When God reveals things about others to me by His Spirit I
   - ❏ become critical.
   - ❏ intercede for them.
   - ❏ share it with others.
   - ❏ other

2. How do I feel about the promise that God will give them life?

3. I must take care to worship God myself if I want others to be right with Him because

APRIL 1

1. A time when I prayed, and God worked wonders was

2. During this time of my life I can describe myself as
   - ❏ one who is burdened.
   - ❏ one who is worshiping.
   - ❏ one who intercedes.
   - ❏ one whose heart is hardened.

3. The Holy Spirit is teaching me to pray for my own family, beginning with

4. As I pray for my coworkers, I want to lift up

5. My country needs prayer in the following areas:

6. Another crisis I want to intercede for is

APRIL 2

1. What the Lord Jesus Christ means in my life today is

2. My ability to explain the purposes of God to others is limited by my
   - ❏ experience.
   - ❏ lack of Bible knowledge.
   - ❏ need to be discipled.
   - ❏ fascination with other things.
   - ❏ lack of passion for Jesus.

3. A time when I received insight into Jesus because of a physical blessing from God was

4. I knew I was more committed to Christ after this experience because

5. Has God revealed the need for a high degree of character in me? Explain.

APRIL 3

1. Does a subconscious pride, even a pride in my religion, lurk in my disposition?

2. I am sometimes guilty of the same sins as the Pharisees, such as
   - ❏ looking down on one who confesses to be a humble sinner.
   - ❏ holding others accountable where I myself have failed.
   - ❏ trying to impress others (rather than God) with my prayers or my giving.
   - ❏ other

3. What can I learn now from closing doors on others?

APRIL 4

1. Has God engineered my circumstances so that I have had this experience of inner desolation?

2. How did I respond toward this internal death to God's blessing?

3. What is God after in me when He withholds the blessings I expect from Him?

4. What is the place of darkness in my circumstances where I do not see God just now?

5. Will I let Him do as He likes?

APRIL 5

1. Gethsemane and Calvary are the gateways into life for me because

2. Jesus' agony, when face-to-face with sin, was that He would

3. I identify (or fail to identify) with His struggle because

April 6

1. Reflect and comment on the following truths:

   The Cross of Christ

   - was really the Cross of God.
   - can never be fully comprehended through human experience.
   - is God exhibiting His nature.
   - is the gate for all into oneness with God.
   - is the reason salvation is so easy to obtain.
   - cost the heart of God all the pain.
   - is the place where God and human beings collide.

2. The Cross of Christ made it possible for me to have fellowship with God. The thing I appreciate most about my fellowship with God is

3. Explain how the Cross is the answer to all my problems or circumstances in time and in eternity.

April 7

1. To what extent does the life of the risen Christ dominate me?

2. In what way have I developed the proper spiritual condition to deal with the words of Jesus?

3. I know of His indwelling in me by the fact that

4. Why is it best not to speak of my mountaintop experience before there is a connection between the vision and the way I live it out?

APRIL 8

1. Our Lord's cross is the gateway into

2. Because of His resurrection, He has the power to convey His

3. I can now know the power of His resurrection and walk in newness of life by

APRIL 9

1. To see Jesus means

2. I know I have (have not) seen Jesus because

3. Do I believe God is big enough because I see Jesus for who He is, or do I believe He is big enough only because of what He has done for me? Explain.

4. There is a division between my friend and me because we do not see Jesus alike; therefore I will

5. I want others to see Jesus even if they don't believe me, because Jesus is

APRIL 10

1. The decision I've made about sin in my life up until now has been

2. It takes me a long time to make a complete decision to crucify sin in myself because

3. What prevents my being radical at this point?

4. Am I ready for the Spirit of God to search me?

5. The thing that lusts against the Spirit of God in me is

APRIL 11

1. A way I am like Jesus is

2. My personal life has been rearranged before God in the following ways:

3. The Holy Spirit has invaded my life by

4. One area I have been reluctant to let Him invade is

5. One way I try to walk in the light is

6. I found the life of Jesus evident recently as I

April 12

1. My part in receiving the sovereign grace of eternal life is

2. Choose the statement that is most accurate and explain why.
   ❏ I can receive the power of the Holy Spirit.
   ❏ I can receive the Holy Spirit.
   ❏ The power is the Holy Spirit.

3. If I have difficulty getting right with God, it is because

4. The decision I want to make today is

April 13

1. Am I able to give God back the responsibility of my burdens?

2. I will roll my burden back on the Lord by

3. One burden of doubt God may not want me to bear is

4. A burden of sin I need to turn over to God is

5. I will cast this on Him by
   ❏ asking God what to do.
   ❏ praying about it alone.
   ❏ getting counseling at
   ❏ requesting prayer from
   ❏ going to a seminar.

1. Match each item with the phrase that completes its thought.

    a. Take my yoke upon you   ___ is my strength.
    b. To them that have none   ___ and learn from me.
    c. The joy of the Lord   ___ He increases strength.
    d. The peace and light   ___ is proof the burden is there.

2. When I feel the pressure of God's hand on me I

    ❏ am invincible.
    ❏ talk with Him about it.
    ❏ complain to others.
    ❏ compare it to what Jesus suffered.

3. One burden in my life I need to talk to God about is

4. I will ruthlessly kick the whine out of my life today by

1. Regarding my spiritual life, I have been paying no attention to

2. Regarding my physical life, I have been paying no attention to

3. Regarding my intellectual life, I've been paying no attention to

4. Because the details of my life matter a great deal to God, I will give more time to my

    ❏ spiritual life.
    ❏ physical life.
    ❏ intellectual life.

APRIL 16

1. In a mountaintop experience, God has shown me

2. I will learn to live in the ordinary day according to what I saw on the mountain by

3. I have tried to do this before, but

4. I will go after it again, and I will

5. I will burn my bridges by

APRIL 17

1. The crisis of abandonment for me is

2. I came up to the crisis externally

3. The internal abandonment came

4. Will I deliberately commit my will to Jesus Christ?

5. At first, emotion may prevent me from making the transaction, therefore, I will

6. I will make the transaction of committing my will to the thing I do see, which is

APRIL 18

1. God called me, and the answer I gave was

2. When God calls me, the answer I will give is

3. My relationship to God means I am

4. Where I am in relation to God's call is

5. My response to obscure duty is

6. When a duty presents itself, and I hear God's call, out of love for Him I will

APRIL 19

1. After I have been through a great crisis in an area, have I noticed that I am able to be tempted in that same area? Why or why not?

2. An area of weakness I need to pray about is

3. The temptation will come in the least likely thing because

4. I need to be extra aware after a great

5. A strong point for me that could become a weakness may be

6. In order to be kept by the power of God, I will

APRIL 20

1. I may be misjudging my spiritual capacities because
   - ❏ they have nothing to do with natural gifts and abilities.
   - ❏ they relate to the gift of the Holy Spirit.
   - ❏ they are measured on the promises of God.

2. God does not expect more than I can give, but the problem may be

3. If I justify myself or worry, I am saying that God

4. Am I critical in the natural or spiritual realm? One example is

5. Do I know some of God's promises? Two of my favorites are

6. Am I open to the Holy Spirit?

APRIL 21

1. It is good to be simple like a child, but not childish. Am I childlike in the way God wants me to be?

2. An example of an opinion I have that makes me dense is

3. I may be hurting Jesus now by asking Him

4. I realize it is not good to be fully aware of what God is doing in me because

5. Other people need to see God manifest Himself in me so that

6. Rather than worry and hurt my Lord when I am troubled, I could

April 22

1. One time when I felt I was standing alone was

2. An encouraging person God allowed to leave my circle was

3. One who used to stand with me, but no longer does is

4. The supreme advantage of having Jesus stand with me is that He

5. The thing that keeps me from looking directly into the face of God is

6. If I look into God's face and then go forth to talk with others, I will

April 23

1. Compare the items in each column and mark which is most true of me.

___ My only concern is to concentrate on God.

___ I worship my work.

___ All the boundaries of life are completely free with the freedom God gives His worshiping child.

___ I am overly burdened by my work.

___ All the limits of my life are free under the control and mastery of God alone.

___ I am a slave to my own limits.

___ There is no longer any responsibility on me for the work.

___ I have no freedom of body, mind, or spirit.

___ I will allow nothing to hinder my cooperation with Him.

___ There is no freedom and no delight.

2. I will stay in constant touch with God today by

APRIL 24

1. Find the false statement.

   As a Christian worker, I

   ❑ realize wanting to be successful in service can be a snare.
   ❑ am to disciple lives until they are wholly devoted to God.
   ❑ must reproduce my own kind spiritually.
   ❑ am to live a life that is a standard to others.
   ❑ am to have a life hidden in Christ.
   ❑ must remember that discipleship is optional.
   ❑ am not to dictate to God or others.

2. As a Christian worker, I will seek the approval of God rather than rejoice in successful service because

3. If I possess the traits of a dictator I will

APRIL 25

1. When it comes to being ready "in season," I am

2. In regard to being ready "out of season," I am

3. Should I wait to be inspired, or just do my best?

4. One time I made too much of a rare moment from God was when

5. The duty that is at hand is

APRIL 26

1. A tradition I once held that misrepresented God was

2. I realized this error when

   I did something about it when

3. I may run into a wrong belief in myself again, so I will

4. I have a better knowledge of God since

APRIL 27

1. One great thing I want for myself is

2. The reason I want this is

3. If I contrast that thing with having an intimate relationship with God, I would have to say

4. The reasons I would want God Himself in preference to just His gifts are

5. Three "right" things I can ask God for today are

6. I get to know God as I ask Him for things by

APRIL 28

1. The awareness that there is something greater than property, possessions, or blessings is

2. I would say this "life hidden in Christ" is the greatest gift of all because

3. The answer to being tired of my life is to

4. The reason I will feel so surprised and delighted when I abandon myself to God is

APRIL 29

1. The way I feel about uncertainty is

2. The end that I imagine I will reach is

3. My life is characterized by
   ❏ common sense.
   ❏ uncertainty seasoned with grace.
   ❏ a sigh of sadness about uncertainty.
   ❏ being packed with surprises.
   ❏ dignity and severity.
   ❏ spontaneity and joy.
   ❏ uncertainty and expectation.

APRIL 30

1. An occasion when love burst forth from me that surprised even me was

2. Later, as I reflected on that experience, I thought

3. I cannot take credit for this kind of love because it

4. I can't really prove my love to God because

5. If I want more love in my heart for God and others, I will need to appropriate it by

MAY 1

1. When it seems that God has sealed up heaven, my response is

2. The value in doing my work as a hidden person is that

3. A self-assured saint is of no value to God because

4. I have greater power to withstand the struggles of my work because

5. My work is my standard and my moments of inspiration are exceptional because

6. The awareness of His continued presence became real to me as I

MAY 2

1. The problem with being caught up in a cause or an issue rather than in the inspiration of the vision of God is that

2. I will know when I have the vision of God because
   - ❏ I will have patience.
   - ❏ inspiration will come with the vision.
   - ❏ things will come to me with greatness.
   - ❏ my life will have vitality.
   - ❏ I will have the power to endure with no word from God Himself.

3. One way I know I am reaching out for more than I have already grasped is

4. If I have the inspiration of the vision of God I have more than I can experience because

MAY 3

1. The reason my sympathy and concern are a deliberate rebuke to God is

2. God's primary interest and concern for others is that they

3. I have a tendency toward bias and sympathy in my intercession for

4. When I stop being identified with God in intercession, it is not because of sin, but because of my

5. God gives me discernment about others' lives so that I will

MAY 4

Intercession is not:
- bringing my sympathies for myself or for others before God.
- demanding that God do what I ask.
- getting irritated with God, or glorifying my own natural sympathies.
- being stubborn, spoiled, irritable or determined to have my own way.

Intercession is:
- remembering that I may approach God because of the identification of my Lord with sin.
- being allowed into the Holy of Holies because of the blood of Jesus.

1. How can I identify myself with God's interest in others, realizing that the identification of Jesus with sin means a radical change of all of my sympathies and interests?

2. Am I willing to give up my own sympathies and substitute in their place God's interests in others?

MAY 5

1. The good news about God, in my own words, is

2. The great thought of God behind the experience of salvation, in my own words, is

3. Judgment is the sign of the love of God because

4. The reason for not sympathizing with someone who finds it difficult to get to God is

5. My responsibility is only to

   The Spirit of God will

6. My self-reliance must die so that

MAY 6

1. Compare the items in each column and mark which is most true of me.

   As I share Christ with others I

   a. ___ demand they believe as I do.　　　___ demand they align their live with Jesus.

   b. ___ bring liberty to their thoughts and opinions.　　　___ present liberty for the conscience of others.

   c. ___ water down the truth of God.　　　___ never apologize for God's truth.

2. I am placing a yoke on another, one that is not of God, by

3. God is in the process of undoing my faulty notion that others must see as I do or they are wrong. The following describes where I am and how I'm doing in the process.

4. The last time I was patient and gentle in regard to this was

MAY 7

1. Some of the things God has done in me are

2. My personal love for Him is

3. If I want to be closer to Him and more devoted to Him I will

4. The conditions I see as strict are

5. The glorious side to all of this is that

6. If I allow the Master Builder to direct and control me completely, I will

May 8

1. One area in my life where I have said, "I can't take anymore," is

2. God's purpose may be to

3. I will maintain my intimate relationship with Jesus by

4. Here are my thoughts about the following kinds of life:

   • Unwavering life –

   • Life that is one great romance –

   • A life of seeing wonderful things happen all the time –

   • A life disciplined to get me into a central place of power –

May 9

1. Do I have revelation (vision) or only spiritual principles?

2. I will guard against acting on my principled understanding alone, and will act on God's revelation instead, by

3. I will regain freshness and vitality in my spiritual outlook today by

MAY 10

1. Three things God will not do for me are

2. I was mistaken in my thinking that God would

3. I need to take the initiative in the following habits:

4. My instruction to myself in the way I must go is

5. I will act in faith on the following decision. In fact, I will make it irrevocable by setting a deadline to begin or finish.

6. I will know when the habit has been formed because when the crisis comes I will

MAY 11

1. Comment on my progress as God works to remove these three things from my life. He doing this with regard to my

   ❏ insincerity –

   ❏ pride –

   ❏ vanity –

2. God didn't love me because I was lovable, but because

3. God has brought people around me I could not respect, and I will

4. I will love the unlovable with His love by

5. Because God has loved me beyond all limits, I will

May 12

1. As I practice godly habits, I am able to prevent a sense of spiritual pride from developing by

2. The missing quality that needs to be worked into my life is

3. Am I so immersed in the Lord that I practice prayer and Bible reading without being visible about it?

4. Am I so aware of my holiness that I place restrictions on myself that didn't come from God?

5. My life will be simple like a child because I will know

MAY 13

1. My human nature struggles with God's commands. If I obey His commands, they actually become divinely easy because

2. The way I continually hold God's standards in front of me is

3. Am I willing to have a sensitive conscience and live in perfect harmony with God's Son?

   If so, the result will be that I will know that good and perfect

4. When my conscience speaks, I must not debate, so that I may keep my

May 14

1. The last time a disagreeable thing happened to me, my response was

2. I will learn to appreciate adverse situations by allowing

3. God can use my circumstances to exhibit

4. The way I feel about discovering a new way of manifesting my Lord is

5. I will keep my soul conditioned to manifest the life of the Son of God by

❏ being active in the Word.
❏ letting the Word be active in me.
❏ maintaining an attitude of praise.
❏ looking for God's approval.
❏ avoiding the fear of other people.
❏ living on the memory of my past experiences.
❏ other

May 15

1. I am to work out my salvation with my speech, my thinking, and my emotions so that

2. The last time I leaped over a difficulty with God's help was

3. Is there a fiery trial in my life at this time? If so, I will exhibit Him in my flesh through this trial by

4. Today I will commit to one of these disciplines. I will

❏ stop complaining.
❏ be ready for anything He brings my way.
❏ manifest the Son of God in my life.
❏ submit to His will.
❏ be broken bread and poured out wine to feed and nourish others.

May 16

1. The last time I recognized God's provision for me was when

2. Why is it not true humility to talk "poor talk"?

3. The time I experienced God removing some of my so-called wealth was

4. His purpose in doing this was

5. God will hold me responsible if

May 17

1. Until Jesus was transfigured on the mountain, He was a perfect

2. After this change, His life became a substitute for mine so He could carry me through three experiences I could never enter on my own. List the three experiences:

3. Match the following truths.

   a. Ascension   ___ 1. Jesus is the door I can enter
                                            to a relationship with God.

   b. Cross   ___ 2. Jesus has the right to give
                                            eternal life to anyone.

   c. Resurrection   ___ 3. Jesus entered heaven and
                                            keeps the doors open to us.

4. I am grateful that Jesus came back down the mountain to

May 18

1. In one way I am like a lily of the field in that I

2. I try to be consistent or useful before others, but I could rely more on God by

3. A circumstance I fear God may fail me in is

Take a minute to focus on Him and practice giving this over to Him.

4. Describe someone who has had an influence on me by living simply and unaffectedly.

5. Reread the last paragraph of today's devotional. Use it to write a brief prayer about my focus on God.

May 19

1. God does not shield me from trouble because

2. A time when I experienced God being with me in trouble was

3. I can be more than a conqueror because

4. As I go through tribulation, my part is to remember that God

5. In tribulation, distress, or even famine, logic is silenced, but some extraordinary thing happens to someone who

6. Where is God when I go through these tribulations? See Psalm 91:15.

MAY 20

1. As I move from my old patterns of thinking to allowing the mind of Christ to be formed in me, the transition will mean that I

2. To possess my own soul with patience means

3. Where I am in this journey of building my own soul is that I'm

   ❏ still at the entrance and not going in.
   ❏ proceeding with caution.
   ❏ jumping in, and I'm going to create and build my soul in accord with the new life God has placed within me.

MAY 21

1. First, number the following in order of importance. Then, in a twenty-four-hour day estimate how many minutes or hours I spend on each activity.

   ___ relating to God
   ___ making money
   ___ being clothed
   ___ being fed
   ___ enjoying life

2. I've made a serious effort to seek God's kingdom and righteousness first by

3. I suspect that my life may be out of His order in the following ways:

4. The dominating focus of my life has been

5. I will begin now to seek God first by

MAY 22

1. My response to the thought of being one with Jesus is

2. The losses, difficulties, and defeats in my life are allowed for the purpose of

3. The affect of these things on me is that I am growing
   - ❏ more saintly.
   - ❏ sweeter.
   - ❏ better.
   - ❏ nobler.
   - ❏ more evil.
   - ❏ more critical.
   - ❏ more fault finding.
   - ❏ more insistent on my own way.

4. Because difficulties in life drive me to a new level of intimacy with the Father, I will

MAY 23

1. Read Matthew 6:25 and reflect on the idea that commonsense carefulness in a disciple is unbelief. One area of worry for me in relation to this is

2. Jesus is trying to squeeze into my life and ask, "Now where do I come in this?" My response has been

3. Confusion in my life has been in the area of

4. My unbelief about God in this area is related to

5. I believe God is saying

6. The area in all of this that I cannot see, where worry comes in, and I need to abandon myself is

May 24

1. How has God revealed Himself to me in His majesty?

2. Did my experience bring with it the delight of despair?

3. My reaction to the vision was

4. When I see or feel the Lord's majesty, I realize that within me

5. I also recognize my limits and allow Him to

May 25

1. Possibilities that opened up to me when I began to live the life of faith were

2. The natural has been transformed into the spiritual by

3. Am I insisting on my rights, to the detriment of my spiritual growth? If so, how?

4. "Good is always the enemy of the best." Good is the worst enemy to my life of faith because

5. Am I willing and ready to walk according to the standard that has its eyes focused on God? I will begin by

May 26

1. Prayer is

   ❏ the breath in my lungs.
   ❏ the blood from my heart.
   ❏ without ceasing.
   ❏ a childlike habit.
   ❏ the life of a saint.
   ❏ powerful if I am obedient.
   ❏ always answered.
   ❏ answered in the best way every time.

2. The last time I was looking for God to answer a prayer in a way that lined up with my common sense was when

3. That which stops my offering up a prayer at this moment is

4. If there is nothing stopping my prayer, I will respond to God about the view of prayer depicted above.

May 27

1. The waiting that was required of the disciples in Jerusalem before the Holy Spirit could be given was for the purpose of

2. The waiting required in my life depends on my own

3. I believe the Holy Spirit is here; this has been revealed to me in the following ways

4. Some things lacking in me or amiss in my attitude that may offend the Holy Spirit are

5. If I want the Holy Spirit in my life, my attitude must be one of

6. I will make an effort today to receive reviving life from my ascended Lord by

MAY 28

1. The last question that separated me from the Father was

2. Matching:
   a. There are many things still hidden from my under standing
   b. When I come to the point of total reliance on the resurrec-tion life of Jesus
   c. I will not need to ask
   d. Until the resurrection life of Jesus is fully exhibited in me
   e. In that day, I will be one with the Father

   ___ I will have many questions about many things.
   ___ just as Jesus is.
   ___ but they will not come. between my heart and God.
   ___ I will be brought into complete oneness with the purpose of God.
   ___ because I will be certain that God will reveal things to me in accordance with His will.

3. Is there a willingness in my spirit to submit to the life of Jesus?

MAY 29

1. Since I don't use Jesus' name as a magic word but rather pray in His nature, I know His nature by

   ❏ hearing His voice.
   ❏ walking with Him.
   ❏ His answers to my prayers.
   ❏ reading His Word.
   ❏ being lifted into heavenly places and learning the teachings of God.

3. I know that my life will have difficulties and uncertainties, but the Father's love will

4. If my relationship with God is untroubled and I have His peace in the midst of difficulties, then I

5. Read the last sentence over until the reality of it causes gratitude in my heart, then thank God that it is true.

MAY 30

1. Has God ever asked me to do something that went against common sense? What did I do?

2. Choose the response that most closely reveals my current experience.

   ❏ I don't want to go against common sense.
   ❏ I'll have faith and take a step in the dark.
   ❏ I want to be adventurous.
   ❏ I will leap by faith into what Jesus says.

3. Write out one of Jesus' statements that seems "mad." Think about this statement until the awesome reality of why God said it finds its place in my spirit.

4. Do I want to be the one daring person out of a crowd to invest my faith in the character of God? If so, tell Him.

MAY 31

Put God First in Trust

1. Are there people in my life I trusted who let me down? My response to them has been

2. I am learning that I need to put my trust in God first, so that

Put God's Will First

3. Rather than rush out to do the work of saving the lost, I need to wait for two things. They are

Put God's Son First

4. My personal life can be a Bethlehem for Jesus by

JUNE 1

1. The result of my last commonsense answer to another Christian when intercession would have been of more value was

2. I give people simple, pat answers to problems that need supernatural solutions because

   ❏ it makes me feel more comfortable.
   ❏ I don't know what else to do.
   ❏ serious commitment to another person in prayer could take years to change some circumstances.
   ❏ other

3. I feel panic or hopelessness for others due to

4. When I look at my own human nature apart from the grace of God I see

JUNE 2

1. I would have to say I am obsessed with

   ❏ nothing.
   ❏ myself.
   ❏ my Christian experience(s).
   ❏ God.
   ❏ thoughts about God.

2. The advantages of being obsessed with God are

3. I will choose one of the following and write a prayer of thanks for what it means for me to be obsessed by God's presence.

   To be obsessed by God is to

   • have an effective barricade against all assaults of the enemy.
   • not allow concern, tribulation, or worries into my life.
   • be at ease in the midst of misunderstandings, slander, or difficulty.

JUNE 3

1. A recent time when God revealed how intimately He knows my heart was

2. Some secrets I believe God has included me in are

3. Do I feel comfortable when I am not aware of God's guiding me? Explain.

4. A time I did not heed His restraint was

5. The outcome was

6. Now when there is doubt I

JUNE 4

1. My thinking makes an enormous impact on my life because

2. If I turn to my own fears my life will

3. If I turn to what God says I will

4. Have God's words, "I will never leave you nor forsake you," found their way into my heart yet?

5. Do I believe God is equipping me for some extraordinary work? Explain.

6. Am I able to live without worry in the ordinariness of life? Why or why not?

JUNE 5

1. The difference between being tempted to fear and dreading something I am facing is

2. The thing in my life I am dreading is

3. When I bring God right into this place of dread I feel

4. In the midst of the situation where I am feeling fear, God is saying

5. Therefore, I can say to myself

6. Even if I am frail compared to what I am facing, if God is with me, together we

JUNE 6

1. Put a *W* before statements relating to my *will*. Put an *F* before statements that describe the *flesh*.

___ Agrees with God (Jesus every time).
___ The profound (essential) element in God's creation of humankind.
___ My natural choices in this are in line with God.
___ God is the source of this.
___ A disposition that renders me powerless to do as I ought.
___ Must be "blown up" with obedience to the Holy Spirit.
___ Says, "I will not obey."
___ Never in agreement with God.
___ Sin is a perverse disposition which entered into humanity.
___ An unintelligent barrier that refuses to be enlightened.

2. An area where I must apply the dynamite in my life is

3. An area where I bring an opposing will up against God's will is

JUNE 7

1. The role intercession plays in my life is

2. Does intercession seem less important to me than other Christian activities because it is a hidden ministry? Explain.

3. The reason the Atonement by the Cross of Christ is central to intercession and to all of life is because

4. Jesus dominates my life to the degree that I

5. In general, my abiding consists of

6. Of all the dominating forces in my life, what exerts the greatest power over me?

JUNE 8

1. Have I needed a storm to send me out into God's purposes, or did I cut the line myself? Explain.

2. I would like to stay tied to the dock because

3. The way I will get out into the great depths of God and know things for myself is

4. A point where I did (not) do something, and my discernment increased (decreased) was when

5. It is dangerous to refuse to learn more spiritually because

6. It is better to discern God's will than to get into self-sacrifice for the simple reason that

JUNE 9

1. Asking is difficult because

   ❏ it shows my insufficiency and poverty.
   ❏ I am not desperate enough.
   ❏ it proves I lack wisdom.
   ❏ I don't want to beg.
   ❏ I don't know what I am lacking.
   ❏ I have the blinders of reason on.
   ❏ I am not interested in my poverty.

2. When I feel terrible, or so many things are coming against me at once that it all seems unreal, then I

3. Is humility an attribute of God? Explain.

4. The next time I have a deep longing that only God can fill I will

JUNE 10

1. Which list below more nearly describes my prayer life? Why?

If I ask amiss
   • I ask for things to fulfill me.
   • I aim to fulfill myself more and seek God less.
   • I utter only a simple, feeble cry after a painful experience.
   • I am satisfied with my own experience.
   • I don't need more of God.

If I ask aright and keep on asking
   • I ask so I get to know God.
   • I narrow my focus, and seek with my whole heart.
   • I allow no self-pity, and I cleanse my hands.
   • I am thirsty for His presence.
   • I draw near to God.

2. I will choose one area of weakness from the top list, and I will pray for a breakthrough.

JUNE 11

1. The reason "coming to the Lord" is the answer to all my questions is

2. Find the one false statement.

   If I will simply come to Jesus

   ❏ my real life will be brought into harmony with my real desires.
   ❏ I will actually cease from sin, and I will find the song of the Lord.
   ❏ He will give me rest and sustain me, causing me to stand firm.
   ❏ He will say, "Do this," or "Don't do that."
   ❏ He will move me out of my listlessness and exhaustion.
   ❏ I will be sustained by the perfection of vital activity.

3. My attitude in receiving all of these blessings is the determination to

4. Personal contact with Jesus changes everything because

JUNE 12

1. I will remain with Jesus as long as

2. Make a brief statement about the following.

   I am allowing the Lord to erase self in my life in the following ways:

   • Self-interest –

   • Pride –

   • Self-sufficiency –

3. Do I have spiritual measles? Explain.

4. Do I want to be a saint? Explain.

5. Do I believe God can make me into a saint? Why?

JUNE 13

1. One comforting thought in God making a holy experiment of me is that

2. The reason a totally surrendered saint is creative is

3. One recent experience when I was amazed at this well of creativity within me was when

4. A natural desire of mine that is a barrier to my coming to Christ is

5. The gift within me I imagined I could give God was

6. My response to the idea of giving up my right to myself is

JUNE 14

1. "Abiding in Christ" means

2. The thoughts that often intrude on my abiding in Jesus are related to my
   ❏ work or school.
   ❏ finances.
   ❏ family.
   ❏ social life.
   ❏ other

3. An area where I have been preventing the abiding, or not inviting Jesus in, is

4. I can abide with Him just as I am, and where I am, without trying to change or rearrange myself because

5. Unless I have learned to abide, I keep myself, and Christ within me, moving at a feverish (distracted) pace by

JUNE 15

1. One important godly habit I am working at forming is

2. Drudgery is a test of my character because

3. Am I willing to do menial tasks as Jesus did?

4. The humble thing God has been prompting me to do is

5. I plan to begin this by

6. The last time I did my ordinary, uninspiring duty to please the Lord, knowing the grace of God was with me, was

JUNE 16

1. Place an *E* for *easy*, or a *D* for *difficult*, in front of each of the following:

___ to die for Jesus sake
___ to be a hero for the Lord
___ to lay down my life for my brothers and sisters in Christ
___ to come down into the demon-possessed valley
___ to lay down my life day in and day out with the sense of the high calling of God
___ to walk in a bright and shining moment
___ to accept the salvation of God
___ to exhibit salvation in my life

2. I need to be able to say, along with Peter, "I will lay down my life for Your sake," because this would be my highest sense of

JUNE 17

1. The results of the last time I was judged or criticized were

2. I lose if I "divide up the strength" of another person in judging him or her because

3. A time when I came to a rapid and wrong conclusion about another, and then realized I did not know the full story, was

4. I am not able to enter into fellowship with God when I am in a critical mood since

5. I am willing to cultivate a nonjudgmental attitude toward others by

JUNE 18

1. The big waves and the windstorms in my life that overwhelm me are

2. When my attention is taken up with these fears my focus on Jesus is

3. If I keep looking to Jesus and maintaining my complete reliance upon Him the worst that can happen to me is

4. The last time I responded to God with reckless abandon was

5. Do I recognize His voice more clearly now as a result of this?

6. Jesus' response to a storm is

June 19

1. As I serve out my passionate devotion to Jesus I am aware that
   - ❏ Jesus said to look after His sheep.
   - ❏ His sheep are to be nourished in the knowledge of Him.
   - ❏ Jesus calls service what I am to Him.
   - ❏ today people are devoted to causes.
   - ❏ Jesus Christ is deeply offensive to the educated minds of today.
   - ❏ if I am devoted solely to the cause of humanity I will soon be exhausted and my love will waver.
   - ❏ a disciple's life appears insignificant and meek.
   - ❏ a disciple's life could change the entire landscape.

2. My greatest strength or weakness in the list above is

3. I will begin to strengthen the weakness today by

June 20

1. The reason trying to be right with God is a sign that I am rebelling is

2. I cannot make a deal with God over my own righteousness because

3. When I stand in the gap to intercede, everything I pray hinges on the Atonement because

4. Jesus has already atoned for my sins; now it is up to me to

5. I would evaluate my insight into God's Word as

June 21

1. It is good that I begin to pray for everything and everyone, rather than always looking inside myself. Some ideas for prayer are

    • items I hear in the news –
    • my government / president –
    • my church –
    • people I work with –
    • my family –
    • unreached nations –
    • people of other religions –
    • people in bondage –
    • strangers, prisoners –
    • other

2. I can come to God freely because

3. Am I sick of thinking only of myself yet?

June 22

1. The thing I understand about this eternal law of retribution is

2. The sins I see in others that really annoy me are

3. The reason these irritate me is

4. Would I like for God to judge me as I judge others? Explain.

5. How long will it take me to break free of being judgmental?

JUNE 23

1. I have not become intimate with grief like Jesus because

2. When I do feel grief I am able to turn to Him since

3. Find the one false statement:

   ❏ Sin is a fact of life.
   ❏ Sin is just a shortcoming (defect).
   ❏ Sin is blatant mutiny against God.
   ❏ Sin, or God, must die in me.
   ❏ If sin rules in me, God's life in me will be killed.
   ❏ If God rules in me, sin in me will be killed.
   ❏ I must bring myself to terms with this fact of sin.
   ❏ Sin is the reason Jesus came to earth.
   ❏ Sin is the explanation of the grief and sorrow in my life.

JUNE 24

1. Matching:

   a. It is not being reconciled to sin
   b. I may talk about the nobility of human nature,
   c. If I refuse to agree with the fact that there is vice (wickedness) and selfishness,
   d. Always beware of an assessment of life
   e. The pure man or woman, not the innocent,

   ___ when it strikes my life, I will compromise with it.
   ___ that does not recognize the fact that there is sin.
   ___ that produces all the disasters in life.
   ___ but there is something in human nature that will laugh in the face of every ideal I have.
   ___ is a safeguarded man or woman.

2. In my human relationships, have I reconciled myself to the fact of sin? Explain.

3. I do not need to be cynical or suspicious because

1. Sorrow is one of the most profound facts of life.

   It is foolish to try to evade sorrow because

   • it may produce a deeper relationship with God.
   • it gives me myself or it destroys me.
   • I can only find myself in the fires of sorrow.
   • If I receive myself in the fires of sorrow, I will not be contemptuous toward people, but I will respect and make time for them.

2. An incident when at least one of the above was true for me was when

3. When I go through the fires of sorrow, I want to come out on the other side of the difficulty with

JUNE 26

1. My part in receiving the overflowing favor of God is that I must

2. If I asked God for grace yesterday, does that mean I have it today? Why or why not?

3. One situation where I find myself in need of God's grace is

4. Write a simple prayer asking God to extend His grace in this situation.

5. Is there any reason to endure tribulation without drawing on His grace?

6. God wants me to be a miracle for His glory, therefore I will ask for

JUNE 27

1. If I lose my personal property and possessions I will have
   - ❏ panic.
   - ❏ heartache.
   - ❏ distress.
   - ❏ the proper outlook.

2. Am I on a mission for Jesus? Explain.

3. Can I live without justice?

4. If even the most devout Christians become atheistic in this matter of justice, what will it take to make me godly in this regard?

5. Would I rather have my deliverance or God's deliverance?

JUNE 28

1. The reason I should not choose to be a worker for God is

2. Has the Lord placed a call on my life? Have I turned aside from this? Do I say I am not suited for this call?

3. My part in all of this is to keep my soul

4. Am I called to testify to the truth of God, or to preach the gospel?

5. Is there the agonizing grip of God's hand on me? If this is the case with me, I need to remember three important factors:

   a. Never

   b. I must be loyal to

   c. Remember who I am

June 29

1. Because I am regenerated (spiritually reborn),
   - if my right hand causes me to sin, I should "cut it off."
   - if I am going to concentrate on God, I cannot do everything.
   - some people will not understand why I can't do certain things.
   - it is best to look lame to the unspiritual.
   - some things may be right for everyone else but not right for me.
   - I am not to use my own restriction to find fault with others.

2. Is it a contradiction for my life to be maimed and regenerated? Explain.

3. My response to the unspiritual person who says, "How absurd you are!" will be

June 30

1. Is there a person I treat coolly? Do I have anger in my heart about this relationship? If I don't confess it quickly and make it right before God what inevitable process will begin?

2. What is the pain, agony, and distress in the process of unforgiveness?

3. Why does Jesus go right to the heart of my being in His determination to make me pure and clean as His child?

4. When I insist on proving that I am right it is usually an indication that

5. If I stay in the light and I don't insist on my rights, if I confess my anger to God, and make things right according to the Holy Spirit quickly, then I will avoid

JULY 1

1. Read Matthew 5:21–26. Being angry and not forgiving another is like having a corner of hell in my heavenly life. Do I? Explain.

2. The Holy Spirit will not give up in this matter because

3. I can describe my prison as

4. Am I willing to have God alter my disposition?

5. My response to God's willingness to tax the last limit of the universe to help me be rightly related to Him and to others is

JULY 2

1. Check the area(s) I most want or need to grow in as a disciple.

   ❏ If my best friend's opinion differs from that of Jesus I will be loyal and obedient to Jesus.
   ❏ My devotion to Christ will be characterized by passion.
   ❏ I will be a devoted bondservant motivated by love for the Lord Jesus.
   ❏ I will depend on the Holy Spirit in me to love Jesus.
   ❏ He will set me ablaze with glowing devotion to Jesus.
   ❏ My life will be characterized by creativity.
   ❏ I will be called "inconsistent."

2. One preconceived idea God had to blast out of me was

JULY 3

1. One of my specific areas of sin God focused on was (is)

2. As God revealed this to me I knew I was

3. Did the reality of being in God's presence come through, or was I more aware of conviction of sin?

4. Did I submit to His conviction?

5. Has God revealed the broader underlying nature of sin in me?

6. The beauty of God's faithfulness in convicting me is that if I cooperate with Him, He then

JULY 4

1. Matching:

   a. Fretting means
   b. It sounds easy to say, "Rest in the Lord"
   c. If this doesn't work there,
   d. Fussing (worrying)
   e. Fretting springs from a
   f. Have I been propping (bolstering) up my foolish (stupid) soul with the idea that
   g. All our fret and worry is caused by

   ___ it will not work anywhere.
   ___ always ends in sin.
   ___ getting "out at elbows," or out of joint mentally or spiritually.
   ___ until I live in tumult and anguish (confusion and agony).
   ___ my circumstances are too much for God to handle?
   ___ determination to get my own way.
   ___ planning (calculating) without God.

2. Am I able to envision having a nature that will not allow me fret? If so, the secret is

JULY 5

1. A time when I made plans without considering God was

   The outcome was

2. Am I in the habit of making plans without considering God? Do I find myself worrying a lot?

3. Does it seem unnecessary to bring God into the everyday issues of my life?

4. Do I make the effort to come to God just as I am?

5. The last time that another treated me in an evil manner, and I forgave and went right on loving him or her was

JULY 6

1. What do I envision myself doing for God in the future?

2. Do I realize the reality of the vision?

3. Has the valley of humiliation been a part of my experience?

4. The purpose of being battered into shape is so God

5. Have I given up? Am I in a hurry about all of this? Why?

6. God will be faithful to

July 7

1. One thing I am making an effort to do that is difficult for me in trying to be my utmost for His highest glory is

2. Some areas I try to practice working out my salvation in practical living are in the areas of my

   ❏ relationships.
   ❏ morality.
   ❏ speech.
   ❏ temperament.
   ❏ other

3. I will choose one to let God work on with me, and write a prayer expressing a higher goal for His glory.

4. I believe a life of worth and excellence is a disciplined life that

July 8

1. What does it mean to me that a person's will is embodied in the actions of the whole person?

2. Why is it always a question of what I will do when it comes to a vision of truth, rather than what God will do?

3. Some of the big proposals and plans the Lord has been placing before me are

4. The reason I must deliberately choose whom I will serve is

5. Write here the proposition that is before me right now. I will simply keep it between the Lord and me and openly declare, "I will be faithful."

JULY 9

1. The one thing I rely on other than God is

2. The person I rely on rather than God is

3. The natural quality within me I rely on is

4. Do I expect God to exhibit His wonderful life in me?

5. How is my weakness a plus for God?

6. Do I believe that unbelief is really sin? Will I believe? If I will, what will I be like? Explain.

JULY 10

1. I see the following traits in myself:

   ❏ I am capable of being spiritually lazy.
   ❏ My objective is to secure a peaceful retreat from the world.
   ❏ I am willing to take steps toward Christ-realization.
   ❏ When I meet injustice, degradation, ingratitude, and turmoil I have a tendency to become spiritually lazy.
   ❏ I use prayer and Bible reading as a quiet retreat.
   ❏ I use God only to gain peace and joy.
   ❏ I seek enjoyment of Jesus, not a true realization of Him.
   ❏ I use active work as a counterfeit of spiritual activity.

2. The last time I was hit in the ribs or stomach by someone full of spiritual activity, my response was

3. Jesus never encouraged spiritual retirement because

JULY 11

1. Am I more self-realized, or is my initiative more directed toward knowing Jesus Christ?

2. Do I divide my life into secular and sacred?

3. One point to which I find the Holy Spirit bringing me back over and over is

4. How am I able to recognize Jesus Christ in my eating, drinking, or washing disciples' feet?

5. Today I will recognize Jesus as I

JULY 12

1. If the church becomes self-seeking, it ceases to be spiritual, and then God's larger plan of redemption is

2. What is God's broader purpose for my realizing Jesus Christ?

3. I will build up the whole body of Christ by

❏ praying for other nations, governments, missions in a broader sense.
❏ the way I interact with foreign people, people of other churches, and fellow employees.
❏ the way I give my resources.

JULY 13

1. One or two heroes God has replaced with Himself in my personal history are

2. Is God able to reveal truth to me?

3. Am I allowing God to conform me to His likeness?

4. Am I willing to pay the price of the vision? Check the most accurate statements below.

   ❏ I will be born again.
   ❏ I am beginning to see the kingdom of God.
   ❏ I only see from the perspective of my own biases.
   ❏ I am willing to let God use external circumstances to bring about my internal purification.
   ❏ I am willing to let my priorities be God first.
   ❏ I am willing to come face-to-face with God, and no one else is taken into account whatsoever.

JULY 14

1. How am I doing with the opportunities to exhibit the Son of God in my life?

2. The last time I was insulted my reaction was

3. Why did Jesus ask His disciples to go the second mile or to turn the other cheek?

4. How does it hurt the Son of God if I insist on having my own rights?

5. What area in my life gives me opportunity to realize the real meaning of filling up in my flesh what is lacking in the afflictions of Christ?

6. Why or how is my Lord's honor at stake in this?

JULY 15

1. Am I overwhelmed with my sense of indebtedness to Jesus Christ? If so, am I willing to spend my life expressing this?

2. When I see an unsaved soul, do I feel a sense of indebtedness to Christ?

3. I would like to bring the evident reality of my relationship to Christ to lost souls by

4. If I view myself as a superior person it will hinder me from

5. If I view myself as a bondservant in my indebtedness to Christ and in my relationship to other lost souls, then I will be more likely to

6. How am I able to be free and to be a bondservant simultaneously?

JULY 16

1. Do I really believe in the concept of God's control over everything?

2. Does this mean that my attitude will be one of perfect trust, eagerness to ask, and an eagerness to seek?

3. If I have the realization that my heavenly Father knows all about each of my difficulties, I will be free to

4. Do I still go from person to person seeking help in my difficulties? The advantage in going to God is that He

JULY 17

1. When I speak to another about the gospel do I use:

   ❏ impressive speech?
   ❏ wooing (techniques)?
   ❏ persuasive speech?
   ❏ my personality?
   ❏ unaided power of God?

2. Eloquence and impressive diction may hinder the gospel of God in presentation by

3. In what way is God there when I present the gospel?

4. Is there anything in my sharing the gospel or preaching that flatters me?

5. I will begin anew lifting up Jesus Christ by

JULY 18

1. Matching:

   a. There is nothing miraculous or mysterious about
   b. I control what I am able to explain,
   c. It is not natural to obey,
   d. There can be no real disobedience, nor any moral virtue in obedience,
   e. If one rules another by saying, "You must do this," and "You must do that,
   f. A person is simply a slave for obeying,

   ___ yet it is not necessarily sinful to disobey.
   ___ unless a person recognizes the higher authority of the one giving the orders.
   ___ unless behind obedience is the recognition of a holy God.
   ___ he breaks the human spirit, making it unfit for God.
   ___ consequently it is only natural to seek an explanation for everything.
   ___ the things I can explain.

2. When I refuse to obey Jesus Christ, why does this result in my moving away from His redeeming power?

July 19

1. One area where I have difficulty with submission is

   - ❑ Once His life has been created in me through His redemption, I instantly recognize His right to absolute authority over me.
   - ❑ It is simply the unworthiness within me that refuses to bow down or to submit to one who is worthy.
   - ❑ God teaches me by using these people who are a little better than I am; not better intellectually, but more holy.
   - ❑ The level of my growth in grace is revealed by the way I look at obedience.

2. Write a brief paragraph concerning the insight I have gained about submission.

July 20

1. Am I able to think of an experience in my physical life when my efforts led to counterfeiting the work of the Holy Spirit?

2. What is counterfeit love, joy, or peace?

3. I experienced an obsession when

4. To what length did I need to go to save my spiritual walk?

5. Why do I refuse to or struggle to trust the reality of God's presence?

6. Have I awakened to the reality that God has been here with me all the time?

JULY 21

1. Choose one to complete or answer.

   ❏ I know personally that Jesus came to make me what He teaches I should be because

   ❏ I know personally that Jesus is more than a teacher because

   ❏ My own response to the Sermon on the Mount has been

2. The place I am now in with reference to the knowledge of my own poverty is

JULY 22

1. During the process of sanctification, one area of resentment pushing against the demands of Christ in my life has been

2. Where am I in the process of sanctification?

3. Write a brief note about what I observe with regard to the following relationships. Have I experienced death in these areas?

   • friends (spouse) –

   • father (mother) –

   • brother (sister) –

   • myself –

4. Am I willing to be known for who I really am before God and others?

5. Am I free of being persistent toward anything except God?

JULY 23

1. Matching:

   a. Sanctification means nothing less than the holiness of Jesus

   b. It is His wonderful life that is imparted to me in sancti-fication

   c. Sanctification is not drawing from Jesus the power to be holy,

   d. The perfection of everything is in Jesus Christ,

   ___ imparted by faith as a sovereign gift of God's grace.

   ___ becoming mine and being exhibited in my life.

   ___ and the mystery of sancti-fication is that all the perfect qualities of Jesus are at my disposal.

   ___ it is drawing from Jesus the very holiness that was exhibited in Him, and that He now exhibits in me.

2. Record one experience that demonstrates the fact that I have begun the slow but sure journey toward order, soundness, and holiness.

JULY 24

1. A time when my motive was good but the outward appearance of what I did may have been suspect was

2. Right *being* exceeds right *doing* because

3. Have I permitted Jesus to place within me a new heredity that exceeds the righteousness of the scribes?

4. A wrong motive that God has shown me and for which I repented was

5. Some work has been done in me by the nature of Christ within me in the areas of

JULY 25

1. Two views of the Beatitudes reveal my usual outlook toward Jesus' words and the reality He intended for them to be in my experience. Compare the items in each column and mark which is most true of me.

___ Soothing and beautiful precepts.

___ Simple, unstartling, and unnoticed statements.

___ Statements of very little practical use in my work day world.

___ The literal interpretation is as easy as child's play.

___ Teachings that come with astonishing discomfort.

___ Truths that contain the dynamite of the Holy Spirit.

___ They are startling statements that produce spiritual upheaval in my circumstances.

___ The interpretation in my circumstances are strict and difficult work for me.

2. The beatitude that produces the most spiritual upheaval in me is

JULY 26

1. Do I resent what Jesus Christ reveals about the awful things in my heart?

2. Fill in the blanks with a positive (+) or negative (−).

___ Jesus Christ is the supreme authority on the human heart.

___ He is not worth paying any attention to.

___ I am prepared to trust the penetration of His Word into my heart.

___ I would prefer to trust my innocent ignorance.

___ I will take an honest look at myself and I will put my innocence to the test.

___ I am open to the rude awakening that what Jesus Christ said is true about the possibilities of evil in me.

___ I am living under the false security of a fool's paradise.

1. Matching:

   a. If spiritual things seem dark and hidden to me,

   b. No one ever receives a word from God

   c. Jesus said, in essence, "Don't (pray) say another word to me

   d. I cannot stand as an impostor

   e. The Spirit of God uncovers my spirit of self-vindication

   ___ first be obedient by making things right."

   ___ and makes me sensitive to things that I have never even thought of before.

   ___ then I can be sure there is a point of disobedience somewhere in my life.

   ___ without instantly being put to the test regarding it.

   ___ before Him for even one second.

2. The area Jesus has been trying to drive home to me is

3. Even at the risk of being thought of as fanatical I will

1. Do I tend to think that obedience to Christ will lead to success?

2. The thing God sees as important, rather than my reaching a particular goal, is

3. What is my vision of God's purpose for me?

4. The problem with having a future goal in mind is

5. Each moment of my life is precious to me because

JULY 29

1. The cloud in my personal life is

2. Does the cloud seem to contradict the sovereignty of God?

3. I am learning to walk by faith in this because

4. Something helpful to unlearn in my life would be

5. As my relationship to God becomes stronger, other people become shadows, and the advantage in this is

6. I will be able to look the darkest, blackest fact full in the face without damaging God's character because

7. The reason my cloud is darker when another shares the place where only Jesus should be is that

JULY 30

1. One person I was deceived about was

2. Now that I am free of deception
   ❏ I am more cynical.
   ❏ I am more critical.
   ❏ I see people as they are (facts).
   ❏ I feel great injury, grief, and pain.
   ❏ I think everything is evil, malicious, and cowardly.
   ❏ I think everything is delightful and good.

3. Am I demanding total perfection and righteousness from the people I love?

4. Am I expecting from another person the satisfaction only the Lord Jesus is able to give? Explain.

July 31

1. I tend to be lazy or careless about

2. An outward expression of my relationship to God that needs to be made right is

3. Has God been bringing me back to the same issue over and over?

4. It is an issue of
   - ❏ the way I worship God.
   - ❏ the way I eat and drink.
   - ❏ wandering thinking.
   - ❏ my independent nature.
   - ❏ other

5. How does patience, carelessness over details, and becoming entirely His all fit together? Explain, or write a prayer about the importance of these three factors in my own life.

August 1

He comes where He commands us to leave.

1. Has God asked me to go? If so was I obedient? Did I deprive my people by staying? Do I believe that Jesus means what He says?

He teaches where He instructs us not to teach.

2. The way I am trying to play God's role in the lives of others is

He works where He sends us to wait.

3. As I wait for God to work my attitude needs to be one of

4. One way I am learning to do what I am told is

AUGUST 2

1. I had the typical view of the Christian life until

2. My experience of being delivered in adversity has been

3. If I am certain that I will face adversity, but Jesus is saying there is nothing to fear, how do I reconcile these two statements?

4. "He gives me life as I overcome" means

5. Some of the strain in my life is

6. The first step I will take to overcome my timidity is that I will

AUGUST 3

1. In the life of our Lord, Jerusalem represented

   ❏ the culmination of His Father's will.
   ❏ joy and success.
   ❏ sorrow and failure.

2. In my life, Jerusalem represents

   ❏ fulling God's purposes.
   ❏ no goals of my own.
   ❏ my decision.
   ❏ the compelling purpose of God.
   ❏ conscious agreement with God's purpose.
   ❏ no awareness of God's purpose.
   ❏ more vagueness of God's purpose.
   ❏ confusion about God's target for me.

3. I'm doing what I think is right, and yet the compelling purpose of God remaining on me makes me realize that

August 4

1. God does not discuss His purposes with me because if I knew them

2. God's friends are people who know their poverty because

3. God cannot accomplish any purpose with people who think they have value to Him because

4. Our relationship with God is the most important aspect of Christianity, and if it becomes damaged

5. Our relationship to God is always under attack because

6. My relationship with God right now is

August 5

1. It is easy to see why we think Jesus' life was an absolute failure, but it was a triumph from God's point of view by virtue of the fact that

2. God's call is bewildering since

   ❏ it can never be understood absolutely.
   ❏ it can't be explained externally.
   ❏ it can only be perceived and understood by my true inner nature.

3. I believe that

   ❏ God knows what He desires.
   ❏ nothing happens by chance.
   ❏ God is sovereignly working out His own purposes.

4. I don't say, "I wonder why God allowed this or that," because

5. If I don't have a purpose of my own then I am able to be more calm because

AUGUST 6

1. Getting into the Cross and identifying with Jesus in prayer means

2. My goal in prayer now is
   ❏ to get answers.
   ❏ to have perfect and complete oneness with my Father.

3. Am I irritated and angry with God? If so, explain why.

4. A time I prayed and received an unexpected answer was

5. A living trophy of God's grace brings honor to God by

6. Do I desire to reach a level of intimacy with God where I become one with the prayer life of Jesus Christ? Explain.

AUGUST 7

1. The Lord's childhood is an eternal fact because

2. The outcome of my identification with the Lord is

3. The idea that "God is my only abiding reality," in my life, means

4. Give an example of how God's direction comes to me personally, moment by moment.

5. Because of my relationship with the Son of Man I see Him in certain circumstances that are teaching me to

6. By allowing Him to have His way with me I will

AUGUST 8

1. Make a statement about how the following are manifest in me:
   - Christ's holy innocence –
   - Christ's simplicity –
   - Christ's oneness with the Father –
2. One area where I may not be simple enough is

3. God's Son is being formed in me in the area of

4. The reason I push Him aside or lose touch with Him at times is

5. The Son of God is praying in me in relation to

6. Am I dictating my demands in some area? Explain.

AUGUST 9

1. I am able to recognize the evidence of spiritual pride in myself by

2. My common sense is being transformed into supernatural sense as a result of

3. The last time I remember enthroning common sense was

4. Common sense does not recognize or identify with the Father because it

5. In what way must I be transformed to worship God?

6. I will depend on Jesus today by

AUGUST 10

1. A time when I interfered with a lesson of suffering in another saint's life was

2. Relate a time when I was strengthened by another saint.

3. I am hindered by sympathy because it only

4. Does sympathy make God look bad? Explain.

5. Self-pity is of the devil because it

6. I must be merciful to God's reputation by

AUGUST 11

1. My Elijah (mentor) is (has been)

2. The purpose of my Elijah being removed is

Alone at my Jordan.
3. The separation, or Jordan, in my life occurred when I

Alone at my Jericho.
4. The sign I have received that God is with me is

Alone at my Bethel.
5. What will I put into practice that I learned from my Elijah?

AUGUST 12

1. When I am afraid I
   - ❏ pray.
   - ❏ have an underlying confidence in God.
   - ❏ am reliable.
   - ❏ turn back to elementary panic-stricken prayers as if I didn't know God.
   - ❏ come to my wit's end as if I don't have the slightest confidence in Him, or His sovereign control of the world.
   - ❏ see nothing but giant breaking waves on the sea ahead of me.

2. If my desire is to produce joy in the heart of Jesus by remaining absolutely confident in Him, in spite of what I am facing, I will need to

3. When I am at the point of breaking, is my confidence in my Lord? Relate one example.

AUGUST 13

1. Matching:

   a. The voice of the Spirit of God is so gentle that unless I am
   b. The sense of warning and restraint that the Spirit gives
   c. And if I am not sensitive enough to detect His voice,
   d. Whenever the Spirit gives me that sense of restraint, I call a halt and make things right,
   e. If I continue to grieve His Spirit, there will come a time
   f. But, if I will go on through the crisis,

   ___ I will quench Him, and my spiritual life will be impaired.
   ___ or else I will go on quenching and grieving Him without even knowing it.
   ___ comes to me in the most amazingly gentle ways.
   ___ living in complete fellowship and oneness with God I will never hear it.
   ___ my life will become a hymn of praise to God.
   ___ when that crisis cannot be repeated, because I have totally quenched Him.

2. Am I attached to anything that continues to hurt God? If so, am I willing to have God hurt whatever it may be?

August 14

1. My last reaction to the Lord's rebuke was

2. The way I am able to know the difference between the Lord's restraint or warning and the devil is

3. When the Lord rebukes me I
   - ❏ become discouraged.
   - ❏ pout.
   - ❏ say, "Oh well, I can't help it."
   - ❏ say, "I'm simply going to give up on everything."

4. Am I willing for God to get me into a state of mind and spirit where I will allow Him to sanctify me completely, whatever the cost?

August 15

1. I have received Jesus, and the following is true of me:
   - ❏ I've only learned through listening to others.
   - ❏ Jesus is my personal Savior.
   - ❏ My spiritual history has as its underlying foundation a personal knowledge of Jesus Christ.
   - ❏ I see Jesus.

2. The difference between seeking for the evidence of God's kingdom and recognizing His absolute sovereign control is

3. The outcome of where I am now in relation to sinning or being obedient to the life within me is that I

AUGUST 16

1. When have I sadly misunderstood Jesus?

2. Is my knowledge of doctrine greater than my understanding of intimacy with Jesus? Explain.

3. When have I stubbornly doubted? Check the statements that are true of me.

   ❏ I am able to relate to the indescribably precious touch of Jesus.
   ❏ I am not able to relate, but like Thomas, I need a personal touch from Jesus.
   ❏ I doubt the personal touch of Jesus that others testify about.

4. When I have selfishly denied Him, have I, or have I come close to, denying Jesus Christ? If so, when the Lord restored me He did so by

AUGUST 17

1. The last time Jesus said something very difficult to me the occasion was

2. Check the statements that apply to me.

   ❏ His words were harsh and unyielding.
   ❏ Then Jesus left me alone.
   ❏ I can't explain it for others.
   ❏ I heard Him say something directly to me.
   ❏ I heard it clearly.
   ❏ I realized the full impact of its meaning.
   ❏ It broke my heart.
   ❏ I went away defiant.
   ❏ I was sorrowful and discouraged.
   ❏ The word Jesus gave me has borne fruit.
   ❏ I prevented His words from bearing fruit.
   ❏ He never threw it back in my face.

AUGUST 18

1. Have the words of Jesus produced sorrow in me and left me with no words with which to respond?

2. One area God's Word points to in my life requiring me to yield to Him is

3. Areas the Lord asks me to rid myself of are
   • personal qualities
   • interests
   • relationships of my heart and mind

4. The purpose of God in this is

5. I am likely to hear one of Jesus' harsh, unyielding statements if I am more devoted to what Jesus wants than I am to Jesus Himself because

AUGUST 19

1. Does the influence of my friends or circumstances destroy my life of oneness with Christ?

2. Is my strength being sapped, or is my spiritual growth slow? Explain.

3. Am I seeing myself as separate from Him as a result of a relationship? Explain.

AUGUST 20

1. Meditate on this.

My Part	God's Part
• I will ask the Lord to put awareness of Himself into me.	• He will be my all in all.
• I will not allow self-pity to awaken in me. I will leave others in His care.	• He will steady me until my completeness in Him is absolute.
• I am restfully certain that God always answers prayer.	• God always answers prayer.
• I won't rely on commonsense methods. I will come to Jesus.	• Jesus says, "Come unto Me, I will give you rest."
• I will turn to Jesus Christ at once.	• He will reestablish my rest.

2. When something is causing disintegration I will think and act on it as something to fight against by

AUGUST 21

1. Consider this.

Self-Consciousness	Christ Consciousness
• Conscious influence is prideful and unChristian.	• True character of the loveliness that speaks for God is always unnoticed.
• If I wonder if I am being of any use to God I lose the beauty and freshness of the touch of the Lord.	• He who believes in Me . . . out of his heart will flow rivers of living water.
• Those people who thought they were a godly influence on me did not actually influence me.	• Those who did not have even the slightest idea they were influencing me did have a godly influence in my life.

2. The difference between deciding for Him and yielding to Him is

3. One person who influenced me in a godly way, who probably didn't know God was even using him or her, was

AUGUST 22

1. Check the statements that apply to me.

   ❑ I am at the end of myself.
   ❑ I am prepared for His coming.
   ❑ I am prepared for Him to drag every wrong thing I've ever done into the light.
   ❑ There is something blocking the way.
   ❑ I know I am not worthy to carry His sandals.
   ❑ I am still trying to defend my actions.
   ❑ God cannot come into my life; I'm not at the point of complete repentance.
   ❑ I am willing to have Jesus Christ perform His work in me.
   ❑ I am conscious of my absolute unworthiness.

2. That which may be blocking the way for Jesus to begin in me is

3. To remove this blockage I will

AUGUST 23

Write a comment, solution, or prayer after each phrase or statement.

1. Prayer is an effort of the will.

2. Select a special place for prayer.

3. I will have a secret stillness before God.

4. I must fight wandering, idle thinking.

5. Am I more sure of God than anyone or anything else?

6. I know that God is in the middle of my everyday circumstances all the time because

7. If I will begin my day opening my life completely to let God in, then

AUGUST 24

1. Check off statements that are true of me. Am I a good child asking for something good?

   ❏ God hears me regardless of my relationship with Him.
   ❏ It is God's will to give me what I ask.
   ❏ I won't faint and give up, but I will find out the reason I've not received.
   ❏ My relationship with my spouse is right.
   ❏ My relationship with my children is right.
   ❏ My relationship with my fellow students is right.
   ❏ I have been irritable and cross.
   ❏ I have the attitude of a good child.

2. My relationship with God is filled with

3. My life is characterized by

AUGUST 25

1. My experience with the joy of self-sacrifice has been

2. Self-surrender is difficult for me because

3. The conditions I have laid out for God are

4. Joy does not result from this because

5. A time when I yielded myself in absolute submission to Jesus Christ was

6. The natural desires I have that could hinder my walk in love before God are

AUGUST 26

1. Check any statement that applies to me.
   - ❏ I am severely troubled right now.
   - ❏ I am afraid and confused.
   - ❏ I've left no stone of my faith unturned.
   - ❏ My life seems completely barren.

2. Peace apart from Jesus is based on ignorance because

3. Do I reflect God's peace? The reason I know this is because

4. Is the face of Christ hidden from me? Explain.

5. I have decided that I will
   - ❏ lay everything out before Jesus Christ and receive His gracious peace.
   - ❏ worry my way out of this problem.

AUGUST 27

1. The vision I have seen on the mountaintop is

2. I have obeyed what I have seen so far by

3. I have not done anything to date because

4. In the matter of sanctification and the light God has given, I am

5. I am working the truth out in my real life in the area of

6. One aspect of my life where I need to face truth and bring it into my real life is in the area of

AUGUST 28

1. I can say that the last time I prayed I came in touch with the truth and the reality of God Himself because

   One truth or reality about God I've learned in coming before Him in prayer is

2. I am able to be myself before God and present Him with my problem because

3. The evidence that prayer has worked miracles in my inner nature is

4. Check the statements that apply to me in relation to prayer.
   - ❏ If I ask I will receive.
   - ❏ Sometimes I complain to God.
   - ❏ I may apologize to God.
   - ❏ I ask with the boldness of a child.
   - ❏ I wait until I am at my wit's end.
   - ❏ I am self-sufficient.

AUGUST 29

1. Matching:

Faith	Common Sense
a. Every time I venture out in faith	___ common sense is more natural.
b. Faith is not common sense,	___ common sense cannot trust Him.
c. Faith relates more to the spiritual	___ the testing of my faith begins.
d. Trust Jesus Christ where	___ while my commonsense life shouts, "It's all a lie"?
e. Will I venture out with courage	___ something in my circumstances from common sense contradicts my faith.
f. Every time my theology becomes clear to my own mind,	___ common sense is not faith.
g. As soon as I say I believe,	___ I encounter something that contradicts it.

2. My faith must be tested, because it can only become my intimate possession through conflict. A first hand experience of this is

August 30

1. My relationship to Jesus Christ is more important than my service for Him because

2. Have I fallen into the trap of rejoicing in how God has used me? Explain.

3. It is merciful of God not to show me how He is using me because

4. Since I am placed in my circumstances by God, and it is my relationship to Him that counts, how should I view my usefulness to Him?

5. How would Jesus fail the usefulness test?

6. Am I able to rejoice because God thinks my relationship to Him is more important than my perceived usefulness to Him? Explain.

AUGUST 31

1. What is the difference between joy and happiness?

   Joy is

   Happiness is

2. Describe my joy at having done the will of my heavenly Father.

3. The joy that Jesus has introduced me to is

   ❏ a deep abiding sense of well being.
   ❏ a flicker of ecstasy.
   ❏ a peacefulness.
   ❏ other

SEPTEMBER 1

1. I must remind myself of the purpose of my life; I am destined to
   - ❑ happiness.
   - ❑ health.
   - ❑ holiness.

2. One desire and one interest that may be consuming and wasting my life is

3. Why must God cause even my right, noble, and good desires or interests to decrease?

4. Will there be a cost for me to have a right relationship with God? Explain.

5. God wants to make me holy so that I

SEPTEMBER 2

1. Why is my Lord's teaching anti–self-realization?

2. How was Jesus characterized by self-expenditure?

3. One way I am characterized by self-expenditure is

4. To me, having God squeeze the sweetness out of me means

5. I will be extravagant in my devotion to Jesus in that I will

6. Is there some particular set of rules that prevents me being totally surrendered to God? Explain.

SEPTEMBER 3

1. The very best of blessings in my life recently has been
   - ❏ love.
   - ❏ friendship.
   - ❏ spiritual blessing.
   - ❏ other

2. This will damage my soul if I do not pour it out to God because

3. I could endanger those I love, as well as myself, by grasping for

4. I will learn to pour out to the Lord now, beginning with

SEPTEMBER 4

1. Am I a missionary? Explain.

2. The following people compete in my relationship with my Lord:
   - ❏ father or mother.
   - ❏ spouse or children.
   - ❏ brother or sister.
   - ❏ my own life.

3. Why do I want Jesus to write the word *Mine* over me?

4. When I become His very own possession, am I responsible for my life? Why?

SEPTEMBER 5

1. As I watch with Jesus I am watching for

   - items of interest as they relate to God's heart.
   - people and circumstances in need of prayer.
   - ways in which God is moving.

2. The reason I watch with no private point of view is that

3. My own particular Gethsemane experience has been

4. This experience has allowed me to relate to Jesus through

5. I will learn to watch with Him today by doing at least one thing:

   ❏ I will pray for one unsaved person that I don't even know.
   ❏ I will pray for one Muslim (Islamic) nation today.
   ❏ I will pray Malachi 4:6.
   ❏ I will

SEPTEMBER 6

1. The obstacles in my life that seem to hinder my usefulness to God are

2. My part in this is to

   - stay focused on the Source.
   - never focus on the obstacle.
   - never allow anything to come between me and Jesus Christ–neither emotions nor experience.
   - believe in Jesus.

3. God's part is to

   - open up wonderful truths to my mind.
   - heal and nourish others through His mighty rushing river in me.

4. Today I will do my part to overcome the obstacles in my life by

September 7

1. My responsibility to maintain a generous-flowing fountain of life for others is to be

2. The way I will remain filled is to

3. Check the statements that describe me now.
   - ❏ I am more like the Dead Sea, always receiving but never giving.
   - ❏ My relationship with the Lord Jesus is not right, because there is something between me and Jesus Christ.
   - ❏ A river continually flows through me.
   - ❏ I stay at the Source.
   - ❏ I closely guard my faith and my relationship to Him.
   - ❏ There is a steady flow with no dryness or deadness.
   - ❏ I look at myself and say, "But I don't see the rivers."
   - ❏ I may be obscure, unknown, and ignored but I will be steadfastly true to Jesus Christ.
   - ❏ I will allow God to help Himself to me if He chooses to start His work through me.

September 8

1. The difference between deliverance from sin and deliverance from human nature is

2. A prejudice in me that can only be destroyed through sheer neglect is

3. One thing I am not to fight over, but only stand still, and see the salvation of the Lord is

4. A theory or thought that raises itself up as a fortified barrier against the knowledge of God in my life is

5. The one thing I understand about turning my natural life into a spiritual life is

6. Why doesn't God make this process easy?

SEPTEMBER 9

1. Which of the following describes me?

   ❑ I am impulsive.
   ❑ I am disciplined.
   ❑ I take every thought or project that comes to me by impulse and jump into action immediately.
   ❑ I am not bringing every thought into captivity but am simply doing work for God that has been instigated by my own human nature.
   ❑ I take every thought or project prisoner and discipline myself to obey Christ.
   ❑ I am criticized and told that I am not determined and that I lack zeal for God.
   ❑ True determination and zeal are found in obeying God.
   ❑ I am committed to Jesus Christ not only for salvation, but also to His view of God, the world of sin, and the devil.

2. As I reflect on the items that describe me, I want to renew my mind in the area(s) of

SEPTEMBER 10

1. The last crisis in my life revealed that I

2. The training ground God uses to prepare me for battle is

3. The closest task which God has engineered into my life just now is to

4. Am I constantly training so I will be fit for battle?

5. My own private everyday worship of God in my own home consists of

6. How could I be a hindrance to others if I do not prepare for the great crisis every day in my worship?

SEPTEMBER 11

1. Do I believe that my seemingly random surroundings were really engineered by God?

2. What have I seen that makes me know that I am God's very special choice for His use where He has placed me?

3. The character I exhibit is that I am
   • willing to do the most menial tasks as Jesus did.
   • able to do the most common tasks and do them His way.
   • able to do dishes, use a towel, tie shoe laces, etc.

4. Why does it take God Almighty living in me for me to do the most menial duty as it ought to be done?

5. If I exhibit to those around me exactly what He has exhibited to me, I will need to change the way I

SEPTEMBER 12

1. Is God taking me through a way that I temporarily do not understand? Explain.

The Shrouding of His Friendship

2. Does Jesus appear to be an unkind friend?

   Is He? Will I hang on to Him with confidence?

   If I do, a time will come when

The Shadow on His Fatherhood

3. When God appears to be an unnatural Father I will

The Strangeness of His Faithfulness

4. Some of these bigger issues at stake may be

SEPTEMBER 13

1. The greatest crisis I ever face is the surrender of my will, and the reason is

Surrender for Deliverance

2. The reason I do not surrender my will to Jesus until I know what salvation means is that

Surrender for Devotion

3. Am I ready to give up my right to myself? Explain.

Surrender for Death

4. Am I eager to maintain unbroken fellowship and oneness with God?

SEPTEMBER 14

1. Matching:

   a. Simplicity is
   b. You cannot think through spiritual confusion to make things clear,
   c. If there is something in your life upon which God has put His pressure,
   d. Bring all your arguments and "every thought into captivity to the obedience of Christ"
   e. We see like children,

   ___ then obey Him in that matter.
   ___ regarding the matter, and everything will become as clear as daylight to you.
   ___ and when we try to be wise we see nothing.
   ___ the secret of seeing things clearly.
   ___ to make things clear you must obey.

2. Is there even a small thing in my life that is not under the control of the Holy Spirit? Describe it here.

3. Since I desire a life of simplicity, I will

SEPTEMBER 15

1. Is there a thought in my heart, about anyone, that I would not like brought into the light?

2. I want to renounce hidden dishonesty in the area of

3. I am renouncing craftiness in the area of

4. I will renounce envy now as it relates to

5. I renounce strife in my relationship with

SEPTEMBER 16

1. One way I have gotten to know God better through prayer is

2. It is conceivable that God will change my attitude in my praying for

3. An area of prayer I know my will is involved is

4. Another area of prayer where my will may not be involved is

SEPTEMBER 17

1. Do I suffer a lower level of temptation because I have not allowed God to lift me to a higher-level walk with Him? Explain.

2. A higher-level temptation that I may face could be

3. My inner nature, or what I possess spiritually, is the reason I am tempted by

4. When I realize the possibilities of my inner nature I am

5. Am I aware that I set the level of my own temptation?

6. A time when God sustained me in the midst of temptation was

SEPTEMBER 18

1. The type of temptation I relate to shows that I am

   • drawn away by my own desires.
   • tempted to lose what God has put into me in being regenerated, namely, the possibility of being of value to God.
   • being tempted to shift my point of view.

2. Which temptation(s) would I not detect by myself?

3. Two points of view I have held in the past that did not bring glory to God are

September 19

1. Will I go on with Jesus Christ through His temptations?

2. When God changes my circumstances I
   ❏ go on with Him.
   ❏ side with the world, the flesh, and the devil.
   ❏ shield myself from some of the things God brings around me.
   ❏ will face my circumstances and continually abide with God.
   ❏ will honor Jesus in my bodily life.

3. The reason they are His temptations and not my temptations is because

4. That which is attacking the Son of God in my life today is

September 20

1. Is the secret of my life hidden in the grace of God so that the supernatural becomes natural in me?

2. Check off the following as they relate to my Godlikeness.
   ❏ I am generous in my behavior toward everyone.
   ❏ I am not generous toward people I dislike.
   ❏ I have fellowship even with those toward whom I have no affection.
   ❏ I let my natural affections rule me.
   ❏ I show forth the grace of God to others in the practical everyday details of my life.

3. A real life opportunity God is giving me now to prove whether or not I am perfect, just as my Father is perfect, is

4. I will pray about this opportunity and thank God for His wonderful power to stay poised in the center of things that create confusion and a flurry of activity.

1. Am I willing to be turned into a servant of God for His own purposes? Why or why not?

2. I was created for the purpose of

3. I want to learn to rely on this tremendous creative purpose of God because

4. Make a brief comment of how God must view the following based on what His Word reveals.

   • prejudice –

   • parochial views –

   • patriotism –

September 22

1. Please comment on each of the following with a brief, personal response.

   My Teacher, the Christ

   • knows me better than I know myself –

   • is closer than a friend –

   • understands the depths of my heart –

   • is able to satisfy the depths of my heart fully –

   • has met and solved all of my doubts –

   • has met and solved all my uncertainties –

   • has met and solved all the problems in my mind –

2. What will it take to enter into the kind of relationship with the Master and Teacher where I am aware only that I am "His to obey"?

September 23

1. Matching:
   a. In the Christian life the goal is given at the very beginning
   b. We start with Christ and we end with Him—"till we all come . . . to the measure of the stature of the fullness of Christ"
   c. The goal of the missionary is to do God's will
   d. A missionary is useful and wins the lost,
   e. The missionary's goal is

   ___ not simply to our own idea of what the Christian life should be.
   ___ not to be useful or to win the lost.
   ___ to do the will of the Lord.
   ___ but that is not his or her goal.
   ___ and at the beginning and the end is exactly the same, namely our Lord Himself.

2. For me, to go to Jerusalem means that I

September 24

1. The preparation process that must be steadily maintained consists of (list at least four key things):

   a.

   b.

   c.

   d.

2. Am I settled and complacent in my present level of experience? Explain.

3. My enthusiasm was put to the test when the Lord asked me to

4. When the Holy Spirit detected a characteristic that would never work in His service, my response was to

1. Meditate on this.

My Part	God's Part
• The caliber of relationship God demands of me is impossible.	• He is the One who does the supernatural work in me.
• Jesus Christ demands not even the slightest trace of resentment in my heart.	• My relationship with Him will bear up under the strain when I am faced with injustice.
• I must never allow the relationship to be blurred or fogged.	• He does the examining, purifying, and testing in me.
• I do not determine to be a disciple.	• Jesus chose me to be a disciple.
• God does not ask me to do things that are naturally easy for me.	• He only asks me to do the things that I am perfectly fit to do through His grace.

2. That which God is asking me to do today that I am perfectly fitted to do through His grace is

September 26

1. The reason God does not want me to bring Him a gift until I have made things right in my relationships is

2. Is there a person I need to be reconciled to before I give my offering this Sunday?

3. Do I object to the intense sensitivity of the Spirit of God in me when He is instructing me down to the smallest detail?

4. The true mark of a saint is that he or she can

SEPTEMBER 27

1. I don't need to apologize for my Lord because

2. What is in us that the Lord sees and wants to hurt and offend until none of it is left?

3. Is the Spirit of God bringing to mind something in me that He wants to hurt to the point of its death? If so, explain why my service to God would ultimately be ruined if this thing went unchecked?

4. Do I believe that serving Jesus Christ is a pleasant thing to do?

5. Briefly explain the strictness of rejection (see Luke 9:58–62).

6. What is the desperate hope that remains?

SEPTEMBER 28

1. Check any statements in which I am willing to continue growing.

   ❏ When Jesus calls a disciple He places personal holiness above everything else.
   ❏ Jesus' primary consideration is that I am willing to give up my right to myself.
   ❏ He means for me to have a relationship with Him in which there are no other relationships.
   ❏ Very few of us understand the absolute "go" of unconditional surrender to Jesus.
   ❏ The look of Jesus transforms, penetrates, and captivates.
   ❏ Where I am soft and pliable with God is where the Lord has looked at me.
   ❏ I must humble myself until I am merely a living person.
   ❏ I must essentially renounce possessions of all kinds to follow Jesus.

2. The main area where my nature has never been transformed by the gaze of Jesus is

SEPTEMBER 29

1. Do I have a compulsion to preach the gospel? If so, would I describe it as a clap of thunder or like a gradual dawning?

2. Does this awareness have an undercurrent of the supernatural in me?

3. Have I ignored the great supernatural call of God to preach the gospel?

4. The place where I began putting in my own ideas or abilities ahead of the call of God was

5. Even if the circumstances are difficult God will

6. My part is to agree so the deeper levels of my life will be

SEPTEMBER 30

1. Is God calling me to something I would have never dreamed? Am I able to relate to the tremendous pain? If so, in what way do I relate?

2. My response to His call is
   ❏ I have seen His purpose.
   ❏ I've said, "Here am I! Send me."
   ❏ God is making me broken bread and poured out wine.
   ❏ I am objecting to the particular fingers He is using to crush me.
   ❏ I am trying to choose my own place of martyrdom.

3. What finger and thumb is God using to squeeze me now?

4. My part is to be brought into agreement with Him by staying and allowing Him to do

5. The benefit of this will be

OCTOBER 1

1. That experience I had on the mountain that will help me with the demon-possessed people of the valley is

2. As I descended from the mountain my thoughts were

   ❏ Oh, I don't want to leave here.
   ❏ How will I transfer this into practical areas in my home, on my job, or at school?
   ❏ I must keep this vital relationship with God alive.
   ❏ I will

3. The reason personal character is more important than useful teaching is

4. Am I willing to let God be the one in charge and to simply cooperate with His purposes on the mountain and in the valleys?

OCTOBER 2

1. A recent time of humiliation for me was when

2. Among the thoughts that crossed my mind, were any of them in reference to the Lord? Explain.

3. God is interested in my walk with Him at the everyday level because

4. The valley of humiliation removes the skepticism from me. Check the statements with which I am able to relate.

   ❏ I was, or am, a skillful skeptic about Jesus' power.
   ❏ When I was on the mountain, I could believe anything.
   ❏ When I am faced with the valley and humiliation I still believe He can do anything.

OCTOBER 3

1. Do I have a desire to be powerful for God's glory?

2. The answer lies in my

3. If I have been trying to serve God without knowing Him, I may have slandered or dishonored Him by

4. The last time I met a difficult case in prayer and nothing happened externally was when

5. My responsibility is not to do the miraculous, but to continue

6. The reason the power of the saint lies in the coming down and in the living in the valley is

OCTOBER 4

1. Check any statements that relate to me.

   ❏ I thank God that I am able to see all that I have not yet been.
   ❏ I have seen the vision of myself as one of the choice ones.
   ❏ When I am in the valley I will not turn back.
   ❏ I am not quite prepared for the bumps and bruises that must come.
   ❏ I am willing to be battered into the shape of the vision.
   ❏ My beatings will come in the most common, everyday ways and through common everyday people.
   ❏ There are times when I do not know what God's purpose is.
   ❏ I will let the vision be turned into actual character because it depends on me.
   ❏ I prefer to relax on the mountaintop and live in the memory of the vision.
   ❏ I thank God for making His demands known.
   ❏ I sulk and pout when God tells me what to do.

2. For me to decrease means that I will respond to God's hunting me down by

OCTOBER 5

1. What am I to do with my heredity of sin?

2. The specific darkness leading to condemnation being spoken of here is

3. This is the nature of self-realization, which leads me to say,

4. The reason this is a serious offense to God is that

OCTOBER 6

1. Meditate on this.

My Part	God's Part
• I had no say in my heredity; I am not holy nor likely to be.	• Jesus Christ is a regenerator who can put His heredity of holiness in me.
• I can begin to see why He says I have to be holy.	• Jesus must do more than tell me to be holy.
• I simply need to agree with God's verdict on sin.	• God judged sin on the Cross of Christ.
• I become aware of my need.	• God puts the Holy Spirit into my spirit and the Spirit energizes me.
• I can live a totally new life.	• Christ is formed in me.

2. If Jesus Christ is going to regenerate me, what is the problem He faces?

3. Have I reached the edge of my need so that I now know my limitation? Explain.

OCTOBER 7

1. Do I see sin in the following ways?

   ❏ Sin is not wrong doing, but wrong being.
   ❏ A sin nature is a self-confident nature.
   ❏ Other faiths (i.e., Islam) deal with sins, Christianity alone deals
     with sin.
   ❏ God made His own Son "to be sin" that He might make the sinner
     into a saint.
   ❏ He deliberately took the complete cumulative sin of the human race
     on Himself.
   ❏ God made Him who knew no sin to be sin for us (me).
   ❏ God placed salvation for the entire human race solely on the basis
     of redemption.
   ❏ Jesus reconciled the human race, putting it back to where God
     designed it to be.
   ❏ Anyone can experience that reconciliation, being brought into one-
     ness with God.

2. Why must I hate sin as Jesus does?

OCTOBER 8

1. Check off the statements that most closely describe my willingness.

   ❏ I will be humble.
   ❏ I will be real.
   ❏ I will not argue or evade.
   ❏ I will not go through sorrow.
   ❏ I will be foolish.
   ❏ I will give up my disrespect.
   ❏ I will not expect God to tell me to do some big thing.
   ❏ I will let that something happen in me.
   ❏ I will ask God to search out the immovable stronghold within me.
   ❏ I will let go, if You will uproot.

2. The difference between receiving answers and coming to Jesus is

3. How will I respond to the hands outstretched to me?

OCTOBER 9

1. Meditate on this.

My Part	God's Part
• I have faith in what Jesus Christ has done.	• The sovereign work is God's.
• I realize that Jesus has made the perfect atonement for sin.	• He saves and sanctifies me.
	• He makes atonement for sin.
• I believe things, not do things.	• He redeems the world.
• I build my faith on the fact of the redemption of Christ, not on my experience of this.	• He rights what is wrong.
	• He purifies the impure.
	• He makes holy the unholy.
	• Redemption is the great act of God.

2. Is my holiness based on what Jesus has done for me, or on what I have done for Him?

3. I will exhibit the Atonement today in one practical (unassuming) way by

OCTOBER 10

1. Matching:

a. We do not grow into a spiritual relationship step-by-step
b. It is a matter of obedience, and once we obey
c. But if we turn away from obedience for even one second
d. All of God's truths are sealed
e. I will never open them
f. But once I obey,
g. If I obey God in the first thing He shows me,

___ "But if we walk in the light," we are cleansed "from all sin."
___ darkness and death are immediately at work again.
___ until they are opened to us through obedience.
___ through philosophy or thinking.
___ the relationship is instantly perfected.
___ a flash of light comes immediately.
___ then He instantly opens up the next truth to me.

2. Do I long to have God reveal more truth about Himself? If so, this will depend on my

OCTOBER 11

1. Check the statements that relate to me.

❑ God has trusted me with His silence.
❑ I am willing to learn how God's silences are actually His answers.
❑ I am still asking Him for visible answers.
❑ I desire an even more wonderful understanding of God Himself.
❑ I am mourning before God because I have not had an audible response.
❑ God has trusted me in the most intimate way with absolute silence.
❑ God has given me a silence; I praise Him, for He is bringing me into the mainstream of His purposes.
❑ I thought God gave me a stone, but He gave me the Bread of Life.
❑ I will allow God's stillness to get into me, causing me to be perfectly confident that He has heard me.

2. Am I able to visualize how my Lord's silence with me is able to glorify His Father? Explain or imagine how He might gain greater glory through His silence now.

OCTOBER 12

1. My way of walking with God during ordinary times is to

❑ know Him better through His Word.
❑ surround myself or seek out people who know God and/or His ways better than I do.
❑ read books about Christians who were/are ablaze with God's purposes.
❑ watch and listen for current trends relating to what God is doing.
❑ pray according to how God is moving.

2. What will be involved for me to get in step with God?

3. Have I experienced my spiritual "second wind"? If so, how did it occur?

4. I have a desire to merge into personal oneness with God and have God exhibit His stride and power through me because

OCTOBER 13

1. The vision of God, or an understanding of what God wants to do with my life, is

2. Have I experienced something equivalent to Moses' forty years in the wilderness? If so, describe the wilderness briefly.

3. Did I feel as if God had ignored the entire vision? Explain.

4. Has God come back to revive His call to me yet? If so, explain.

5. I can only be radiant for God by

6. The right individual perspective is

OCTOBER 14

1. Fill in the Blanks

Me and Missions	Christ and Missions
• Our Lord does not _____ my endeavors.	• He says, "Go," on the basis of the revealed truth of His _____.
• I teach and preach out of my _____ with Jesus Christ.	• Jesus supplies the _____.
• I must _____ Him myself.	• He _____ upon Himself the work of sending us.
To "go" means to _____.	• God's _____ engineers our goings.

2. In what ways do I count my life as dear to myself?

3. I will overcome this by

OCTOBER 15

1. What does it mean to me personally to have the Lamb of God take away my sins?

2. What does it mean to me that Jesus took God's wrath for me?

3. Explain why the following are not limitless:

   Healing –

   Saving –

   Sanctifying –

4. Explain why "The Lamb of God who takes away the sin of the world" is limitless.

OCTOBER 16

1. Choose the statements that relate to me.

   ❏ As a missionary I would be willing to pray rather than work.
   ❏ Work for God, as I do it, shifts my focus from God.
   ❏ I believe prayer is not practical, but absurd.
   ❏ Common sense tells me that compared to work prayer is foolish.
   ❏ I am learning to pray without regard to persons.

2. Do I use distress and conviction to make God look good or bad in the eyes of the lost?

3. Why do we spend so much time working rather than praying and reaping a harvest for our Lord?

4. Am I willing to be His laborer, to labor in His way, and to be sent out?

OCTOBER 17

1. Please place a *T* before all true statements.

___ Prayer equips me for greater work.
___ Prayer is the greater work.
___ Prayer is a commonsense exercise of my higher power.
___ Prayer is the working of the miracle of redemption in me, through the power of God.
___ Prayer is the battle.
___ Prayer is my duty.
___ Prayer makes the ideas of my Master possible.
___ Prayer is a labor that always gets results.

2. The difference between the prayer of a child and of a "wise" adult is

3. Prayer is the battle because

4. Am I willing to be the answer to my own prayer (see Matthew 9:38)?

OCTOBER 18

1. To identify myself with God's interests in His sheep means that I am willing to serve them by

2. As I read 1 Corinthians 13:4–8 I immediately see that I am weak in the area of

3. My love for Jesus is being worked out in practical ways for His sheep by

4. My love for God's sheep, from a commonsense point of view, may appear to be powerless; one example of this is

OCTOBER 19

1. Am I involved in a work that calls itself Christian, but in actuality resembles the world system more than it glorifies God?

2. Am I involved in this endless activity, but have no private life with God?

3. My personal plan for getting rid of the plague of pressure, rushing, and tremendous activity is to

4. I am to be like my Master; therefore I need to develop my innermost life, which reveals His power, so I will

5. Do I take time to immerse myself in the truths of God to soak in them before Him? If so, when the stress and strain comes I will

OCTOBER 20

1. Check the statements that apply.

   ❏ I know God is willing to sanctify me.
   ❏ It is my will to be sanctified.
   ❏ I will make it a matter of action to let God do in me everything that has been made possible through the Atonement.
   ❏ I am willing to let Jesus' life be exhibited in my human flesh.
   ❏ I will receive Jesus Christ to become sanctification by absolute, unquestioning faith.

2. An area in my attitude where I need Jesus to come in and sanctify me to make me profoundly humble is

3. Have I an amazing realization of the love of God for me even when I cared nothing about Him? If so, explain.

4. Since He completed everything for my salvation and sanctification, my part in receiving it all is to

OCTOBER 21

1. The last time I wanted to vindicate myself because the Spirit of God brought feelings of self-conscious foolishness was when I

2. *Spoil* can mean "to impair the disposition of by overindulgence." Am I spoiled? Explain.

3. Am I willing to have any trace of impulsiveness trained into intuition through discipline?

4. Explain why discipleship is built on the supernatural grace of God.

5. Walking on dry land for me means

OCTOBER 22

1. Am I asking God to reveal Himself to me now?

2. If He does not, the reason may be that
   - ❑ I have not done as He asked.
   - ❑ I am in the way.
   - ❑ I will not abandon myself to Him totally.
   - ❑ He cannot witness to me.
   - ❑ He must witness to His own Spirit in me.
   - ❑ I must stop my disrespectful debating with God.
   - ❑ I need to abandon reasoning and arguing.
   - ❑ I will tell Him He cannot deliver from sin.
   - ❑ I am in darkness and uncertainty.

3. If I want the witness, I will throw overboard my

October 23

1. Am I willing to see my prejudices put to death?

2. Our Lord never tolerates our prejudices because

3. Prejudices have to do with my old life because they relate to

4. One way I have seen Jesus remove a prejudice from me is

5. Is there anything of the old life I am not willing to give up? Explain.

6. Am I willing to give up even God's blessing?

October 24

1. I develop an outlook that is not finite by

2. For what reason is no outside power able to touch this proper perspective?

3. My one purpose is to be

4. Why are these perspectives too small?
   "I am standing all alone, battling for Jesus."

   "I have to maintain the cause of Christ and hold down this fort for Him."

5. In what ways is this idea being worked out in me?

OCTOBER 25

1. Do I often wish I were somewhere else?

2. What purpose has God given me that makes me an extraordinary person?

3. My purpose intellectually is

4. The purpose in my heart is

5. The purpose of God's grace and Word in me is to

6. Has God placed His call on me? Explain.

OCTOBER 26

1. Matching:

   a. A missionary is someone sent by Jesus Christ
   b. The great controlling factor is not the needs of the people
   c. The source of our inspiration in our service for God is behind us,
   d. The tendency today is to put the inspiration out in front
   e. But in the New Testament the inspiration is put behind us,
   f. The goal is to be true to Him,

   ___ not ahead of us.
   ___ to sweep everything together in front of us and make it conform to our definition of success
   ___ to carry out His plans.
   ___ but the command of Jesus.
   ___ just as He (Jesus) was sent by God.
   ___ and is the Lord Jesus Himself.

2. My view of people who are foolish enough to trust God is that they are

3. Am I one of those foolish trusters? Explain

OCTOBER 27

1. I am not able to save a soul because

2. But, I am able to

3. The disciples rejoiced that demons were subject to them because

4. If their relationship was not right with God then

5. As a missionary, if I am true to God and His call, will I be a success? Explain.

OCTOBER 28

1. I am saved by

   ❏ believing.
   ❏ repenting.
   ❏ realizing what God has done in Jesus Christ.

2. The cause of my being saved is

   ❏ obedience.
   ❏ consecration.
   ❏ prior to all of that, Christ died.

3. How secure is my justification and sanctification as I receive what Christ has done for me?

4. Am I encouraged by the supernatural miracle of God to change sinful men and women into new creations? Explain.

OCTOBER 29

1. Check the true statements.

   ❏ Jesus died for my sins out of sympathy.
   ❏ By identification He was made to be sin.
   ❏ My sins are removed because Jesus was obedient to His Father.
   ❏ I am acceptable to God because I have obeyed.
   ❏ Jesus came to reveal the Father
   ❏ Jesus came to take away the sins of the world.

2. The revealing of the Fatherhood of God is for those who already know the Son because

3. Jesus spoke of Himself as a stumbling block because

4. Am I determined to have Christ formed in me? Why or why not?

OCTOBER 30

1. Is there a way my faith is in active opposition to common sense?

2. What is meant by "revelation sense," or a sense of revelation? What does this have to do with faith?

3. My ideal faith becomes real by

4. Why does praying through the Word, in faith, work so well?

5. A recent circumstance God used to educate my faith was

6. Why must I know Jesus in order to have faith in God?

OCTOBER 31

1. Relate a time when, as a new believer, God rewarded my faith.

2. In what way(s) has God withdrawn His conscious blessings to teach me to walk by faith?

3. The difference between a life of faith and a life of sentimental enjoyment of His blessings is

4. Where am I in relation to God's character? Do I still doubt His goodness? If so, explain.

5. Have I experienced times of unbroken isolation in the working out of my faith to date?

NOVEMBER 1

1. Two reasons for my not having a private life are

2. In what way has my private life been broken up?

3. In what ways has my life become open, or a thoroughfare, for the world?

4. My view of this openness is

5. Being called into fellowship (intimacy) with the gospel means

6. If I refuse to do this, I actually become a hindrance and of no value because

November 2

1. Do I appreciate the fact that the Lord is a gentleman? If so, why not tell Him.

2. To obey Him out of oneness of spirit means

3. The Lord always gives me an option because

4. I need to deny myself if I follow Him because

5. It is necessary to remember who is asking me to deny myself because He

6. A time when I hesitated to obey was

November 3

1. The way I feel about having the hard outer layer of my individual independence from God broken is

2. When I am liberated from myself and my nature, into oneness with and absolute loyalty to Jesus, what misunderstanding will I be free of?

3. Following is an account of a time when I was loyal to Christ, and I did something for His sake alone.

NOVEMBER 4

1. The way I give people the opportunity to act on the truth of God is

2. I leave the responsibility with the individual because if I don't

3. It must be the individual's own deliberate act because

4. Does my message lead the person to action?

5. After action a change begins due to

6. The "folly of truth" that stands in the way is

NOVEMBER 5

1. I believe that God is taking me through experiences to make me useful in His hands. Some of these experiences deal with

   ❑ wounded people.
   ❑ angry people.
   ❑ critical people.
   ❑ brothers and sisters in Christ who turn on me.
   ❑ others

2. I am beginning to understand what takes place in the lives of others better because

3. My point of view about suffering is

   ❑ I avoid it at all cost.
   ❑ it is inevitable.
   ❑ it deepens me as a person.
   ❑ it gives me a better understanding of Jesus.
   ❑ other

1. I believe

   ❏ in the power available to Jesus.
   ❏ Jesus can heal.
   ❏ Jesus has a special intimacy with God.
   ❏ whatever Jesus asks God, God will do.
   ❏ I need a closer personal intimacy with Jesus.
   ❏ my theology has its fulfillment in the future.
   ❏ I am willing to have Jesus draw me in until my belief becomes an intimate possession.
   ❏ the personal inheritance is mine.

2. Here is what I believe about commitment in each of these areas.

   • Intellectual learning –

   • Personal belief –

   • Intimate personal belief –

November 7

1. Do I believe that my circumstances are ordained by God, and that there is no such thing as chance? If so, then what does this mean to me?

2. One circumstance I have been in, but could not understand why, is

3. What is one purpose of my interceding where God has placed me?

4. Am I bringing everyday circumstances and people before His throne? Share a few here.

5. What is God able to do as I cooperate with Him in this?

6. In what way am I being vague or unsure in my intercession?

November 8

1. Please place a *T* before all true statements.

___ I am energized by the Holy Spirit for prayer.
___ I know what it is to pray in accordance with the Spirit.
___ The Holy Spirit prays prayers in me I can't utter.
___ God searches my heart to know the prayers of the Holy Spirit in me.
___ The Spirit uses my nature as a temple to offer His prayers of intercession.
___ The Spirit of God will not allow me to use my body for my own convenience.
___ The Holy Spirit will be responsible for the unconscious part of me.

2. Do I live as if I realize my body is the temple of the Holy Spirit?

3. Do I keep my body undefiled? Refer to Galatians 5:19–23.

4. Since I must guard the conscious part of myself, I may need to make a change in the area of

November 9

1. I am a sacred go-between in the sense that I am sharing the Gospel with

2. In what way(s) am I so closely identified with my Lord and His redemption that Jesus Christ is able to bring His creating life through me?

3. As I share the gospel I need to make sure I am living in harmony with God so that

4. The problem of the appeal being on the person speaking rather than on the gospel of God is

5. If the person speaking is truly identified with Jesus the message will be valuable in that it will

6. If I want to be used to change the lives of others, as I share Christ with them, then I must first be concerned about my

November 10

1. Do I have difficulty stating the purpose of my life?

   If I do, the reason may be

2. Has God moved me into His purpose?

3. God is able to use me throughout the world
   • by intercession.
   • by sending me.
   • by my sending others.

4. I barricade God from using me if I

5. The personal interests and ambitions I am maintaining now are

6. I am aligned, or identified, with God's interests in the area(s) of

November 11

1. The last time I debated with God the outcome was

2. Even when I know I should, I find excuses for not

3. Do I have the desire to climb to the heights God reveals?

4. Is there a sacrifice of my will that must be worked through?

5. The problem in conferring with others, when we know what God is requiring, is

6. When I try to work it out with my own understanding I am really trying to

NOVEMBER 12

1. Consider this.

Old Things	A New Creation
• I no longer look at these old things the same way. • These old things have lost their power to attract me. • If I still yearn for the old things, it is absurd to talk about being born from above; I am deceiving myself.	• My life had dramatically changed. • My desires are new; God has changed the things that really matter to me. • If I am born again, the Spirit of God makes the change very evident in my real life and thought.

2. I have noticed that my response in a crisis is

3. This action is the result of

4. I am freed completely because

NOVEMBER 13

1. Because I am battling my way into absolute devotion, here is a statement about how I am dealing with each of these areas.

• moods –

• feelings –

• emotions –

2. What are the true facts about Jesus Christ that allow me to abandon myself to Him in complete devotion, without depending upon my own experiences?

3. My fears are

4. I create my own fears because

November 14

1. Am I in the habit of continually asking for guidance?

2. When I feel an inner conflict, what is the Spirit of God saying to me?

3. The last time the Spirit warned me, did I stop? Explain what happened.

4. I am able to renew my mind by

5. I am able to discern God's will when I

6. The last time I saw God in the details of my life was

November 15

1. The last time I interfered in the life of another was

   The outcome was

2. I must learn not to hinder what God is doing in the lives of others because

3. Is there stagnation in my spiritual life? The reason is

4. When God is asking me to advise another He will

5. If I have a desire to be a blessing to other souls I must be

NOVEMBER 16

1. Meditate on this.

Heroic Impressions	Heroic Actions
• I go through a crisis grandly.	• I glorify God when there is no witness, no limelight, no one paying the least attention.
• I say, "I have had a wonderful call from God."	• I do the meanest duty to the glory of God.
• I want others to admire my piety.	• The Holy Spirit has made me so humanly His that I am utterly unnoticeable.
• Success is the test.	• Faithfulness in real life is the test.

2. The humbling human relationships and conditions God is using in my life to glorify Himself and to teach me faithfulness are

3. How am I doing?

NOVEMBER 17

1. What reality of God did Abraham understand in his willingness to trust God and offer Isaac (see Genesis 12:2–3 and Genesis 22:5)?

2. Is my goal God Himself at any cost? Explain.

3. What I understand about God's way, and submitting to God, so far are

4. When Jesus says, "Come," I

5. When He says, "Let go," I

6. When He says, "Trust God in this," I

7. My obedience (disobedience) reveals that I

NOVEMBER 18

1. How are these things keeping me from getting to God?
   • sin –

   • my individuality –

   • wrong thinking –

2. The thing that keeps me from offering myself to God is

3. I tend to
   ❏ aid and assist God.
   ❏ stand against Him and say I can't do that.

4. The difference in being made free from the inside out rather than from the outside in is that

NOVEMBER 19

1. The difference between conviction of sin and being disturbed because I have done wrong things is

2. In conviction of sin the Holy Spirit makes me aware of only one relationship because

3. That which alone enables God to forgive my sin is

4. The price paid for my sin by each of the following was
   Jesus –

   God –

5. The only basis upon which God can forgive sin and satisfy His conscience is

NOVEMBER 20

1. Matching:

a. The only ground on which God can forgive us

b. To base our forgiveness on any other ground

c. Forgiveness, which is so easy for us to accept,

d. Forgiveness is

e. The cost to God was

f. To forgive sin, while remaining a holy God,

g. The revealed truth of God is that without the atonement

___ cost the agony at Calvary.

___ is the tremendous tragedy of the Cross of Christ.

___ is unconscious blasphemy.

___ the Cross of Christ.

___ the divine miracle of grace.

___ He cannot forgive–He would contradict His nature if He did.

___ this price had to be paid.

2. That which I understand about being held as in a vise, or constrained by the love of God, is

NOVEMBER 21

1. The reason the death of Jesus Christ is the fulfillment in history and is the very mind and intent of God is

2. Jesus' death was not martyrdom because

3. Life here on earth without God's plan and it's fulfillment would be

4. If I leave the Cross of Christ out of the story of God's forgiveness

November 22

1. The shallow things in life are

   - ordained by God.
   - not a sign of being sinful.
   - eating and drinking.
   - walking and talking.
   - are equally as important as the profound things.
   - also things that Jesus did as the Son of God on earth.
   - a part of the commonsense life.

2. The reason to show the depth of my life to God alone is

3. Am I nauseatingly serious? If so, why?

4. If I take no one seriously except God how will it change me, or my personality?

November 23

1. The last time I did damage to my own Christian state of mind was when

2. Did I act treacherously in thought or action? If so, explain.

3. I saw the tremendous effects of my wrong state of mind, and the outcome was

4. The power that lies behind this state of mind is

5. A few "cares of this world" which produce a wrong state of mind in me are

6. Do I use the discernment God gives me to criticize others or to intercede on their behalf?

NOVEMBER 24

1. Are my eyes focused on God?

2. The knowledge I am gaining about His countenance is

3. Has God revealed Himself to me? If so, what understanding do I have of Him?

4. Is my spiritual strength being drained because I am not lifting my eyes to God? If so, where has my focus been instead?

5. Is there something coming between me and God? If so, I will change it at once by

NOVEMBER 25

1. Meditate on this.

External–Secular

- The newly born again still lives in this world, so his or her emotions about spiritual life appear unrelated.
- The apostle Paul could let his external life change without internal distress because he was rooted and grounded in God. He lived in the (foolish) basement. His critics lived in the (rational) upper level.
- In secular history the Cross has little or no value.

Eternal–Spiritual

- When a person has emotions about his or her new birth, they are consistent with the spiritual world.
- Paul was consistent about the agony of God in the redemption of the world, or the Cross of Christ.
- From God's or the biblical point of view it is more important than all the empires that ever existed.

2. What do I believe about the external world and the foundation of the Cross of Christ? State your beliefs to yourself again here.

November 26

1. If I want to know the power of God I must dwell on the tragedy of God, the Cross of Christ, because

2. Do I want God's power? In what ways am I willing to break free from my concern over my own spiritual condition and with a completely open spirit consider the tragedy of God?

3. Record here any observations after at least a week of considering the tragedy of God.

4. I will remember to focus continually on the Cross as my source of spiritual energy by

5. Why will people never be the same after hearing about God's focal point, even if they seem to pay no attention?

November 27

1. I believe Jesus Christ is interested in

2. God is not asking me to become a recluse because

3. He is also not requiring me to be a fanatical holy person practicing self-denial since

4. How is it that I can be a part of society and yet be disconnected?

5. If I dwell on the Cross of Christ will I, in a spiritual sense, live in another world? Explain.

6. In the balance of mixing socially in the everyday world as Jesus did, and maintaining my consecration of spiritual power, how am I doing?

November 28

1. The gospel awakened an intense longing in my soul when I was

2. I also had intense resentment toward the gospel in relation to

3. I realize that I cannot earn anything from God through my own efforts because

4. Have I come to the knowledge that I am destitute? If so, briefly explain.

5. Why would having an awareness of being destitute be the greatest blessing?

November 29

1. Please place a *T* before each true statement and an *F* before each false statement. What I have seen of holiness movements, or similar experiences, today is

___ they lack the rugged reality seen in the New Testament.
___ they do not appear to need the death of the Lord Jesus.
___ a pious atmosphere of prayer and devotion.
___ they did not cost the sufferings of God, nor are they stained by the blood of the Lamb.
___ they are not sealed by the Holy Spirit as being genuine.

2. Do I have a personal, passionate devotion to the person of Jesus Christ?

3. Have I been taught the idea that He is only my pattern or example?

4. Do I believe He is salvation itself, and that He is the gospel of God?

November 30

1. Do I speak about my own inabilities?

2. Has God overlooked me?

3. Is it really humble to complain about my incompetence?

4. Is it impossible for God to save and sanctify me?

5. Am I willing to accept God's point of view that His grace toward me was not in vain?

6. To allow Him to be my all in all means that

December 1

1. My life is a tragedy because
   - the moral law does not consider my weakness as a person.
   - the moral law demands that I be absolutely moral.
   - the moral law is ordained of God, and never excuses my short comings.
   - I was alive without the awareness of the law, but when I became aware of God's standard, I realized my sin, and sin leads to death.
   - until I get to this place of no hope in myself, the Cross of Christ remains absurd to me.
   - conviction of sin makes me hopeless, fearful, and confined by the law.
   - I can get right with God only through the death of Jesus Christ.

2. When I choose to obey Him, He will go to the ends of the earth to aid me because

DECEMBER 2

1. Is there a part of me that is trying to be God's perfect specimen?

2. How are being sick, being bruised of God, and living my life for the determined purpose of God related to one another?

3. Is my relationship with God true even in the midst of what seem to be unimportant details of life?

4. When I obeyed the call of Jesus Christ, two of the things I had to do that seemed pointless were

5. Does it seem that other people are living perfectly consistent lives? Give one example.

6. Am I left with the impression that God seemed unnecessary? Explain.

DECEMBER 3

1. Meditate on this.

Of Human Wisdom	Of Spirit and of Power
• I will substitute my knowledge of the way of salvation instead of	• having confidence in the power of the gospel.
• I hinder people (from)	• reality.
• While I proclaim my knowledge of the way of salvation	• I myself must be rooted and grounded by faith in God.
• Never rely on the clearness of your presentation;	• Make sure you are relying on the Holy Spirit, and God's redemptive power, and He will create His own life in people.
• If my faith is in experiences, anything that happens is likely to upset that faith.	• Once I am rooted in reality, nothing can shake me.
• God disapproves of my human efforts to cling to the concept that sanctification is merely an experience.	• Nothing can ever change God or the reality of redemption.

2. Will I deliberately give my sanctified life to God for His service?

December 4

1. Life without war in the natural realm is impossible because

2. Life without war in the supernatural realm is also impossible because

3. How must I fight in the following ways?

  • physically –

  • mentally –

  • morally –

  • spiritually –

December 5

1. What does God's grace have to do with the way I treat my body?

2. How do working out my salvation, and my body being the temple of the Holy spirit, relate?

3. Do I rule over my thoughts and desires? Is this important? Why?

4. Am I more severe in my judgement of others than of myself? Why or why not?

5. Am I willing to present my body as a living sacrifice?

6. What change is the Holy Spirit asking me to make today?

December 6

1. Consider this.

My Question	God's Answer
• Why doesn't God save me? • Why doesn't God do everything I ask?	• He has provided for my salvation, but I must enter into a relationship with Him. • He has done it. The point is will I step into a covenant relationship with Him?

2. I must enter into a relationship with God on the basis of His covenant to receive from Him because

3. When God does something in me, do I focus on what He did, rather than on Him? If I do, why would God not be pleased?

4. The basis of my relationship with God needs to be

December 7

1. Conviction of sin is rare because

2. An understanding of God comes after, not before, conviction of sin because

3. You and I cannot bring another person under the conviction of sin because

4. The Holy Spirit brings us under conviction of sin by

5. Conviction of sin is different from remorse because

6. How does this pattern of conviction of sin, forgiveness, and holiness fit the description of what has happened, and is happening in my life?

DECEMBER 8

1. Feeling sorry for my sins could never have resulted in them being forgiven because

2. Not only does God forgive my sins but He also

3. My response as I realize the depth of what Jesus has done for me is

4. God's real heart has made plenty of entrance available to me if I come

5. This way seems narrow to me because it means I identify with

6. God is justified in saving bad people but He does not leave them sinful because

DECEMBER 9

1. What good things in my natural life hold me back from God's highest?

2. When I overcome my weakness, what I want to accomplish for God is

3. Check the true statements.

   God's highest and best for me is to

   ❏ work for Him.
   ❏ give up my rights and independence to Him.
   ❏ live to please myself.
   ❏ live to please others.

DECEMBER 10

1. One example of the natural life being turned into the spiritual is

2. The area I am working on now, in the natural, through sacrifice, is

3. Am I willing to pay whatever it may cost in my deliberate commitment of myself to God? Explain.

4. My natural life defies the life of the Son of God in me and produces turmoil in me in the following ways:

5. If I do not discipline myself in the problem area(s) above, my entire personal life will be ruined for God because

DECEMBER 11

1. In some way I
   - shove others aside by
   - separate others out by
   - isolate others by

2. I am isolated because I confuse individuality with spirituality by

3. I have noticed the Holy Spirit narrowing my focus and dealing with me in the area of

4. Since I want my spiritual life to emerge I will
   - ❑ be reconciled to my brother or sister.
   - ❑ forgive.
   - ❑ believe.
   - ❑ surrender to God.
   - ❑ other

December 12

1. Check the true statements.

   My personality

   ❏ is limitless.
   ❏ is distinct from everyone else.
   ❏ is too vast to comprehend.
   ❏ has great depths.
   ❏ is the characteristic mark of the inner spiritual being.
   ❏ merges.
   ❏ responds to love.

2. A recent experience when I recognized that I do not actually know myself as well as I thought was

3. I believe I have reached my true identity because

4. The relationship in my life that most resembles Jesus' relationship with His Father is

December 13

1. Redemption is one of the primary objectives of intercession, because without it the person we are praying for is

2. Sympathy in intercession is useless, or worse, because

3. The circumstance that seems to be crashing in on me now is

4. I am being changed in my attitude toward the person or the circumstance in the following ways:

5. God's heart for the person, or persons, is

6. Do I know so much about the situation that I am overwhelmed and can't pray? Explain.

December 14

1. When I experience personal difficulties I

   ❏ always blame God.
   ❏ am tempted to blame God.
   ❏ realize that I am to blame or that it is the result of living in a fallen world.
   ❏ wait to see how God will work it out and glorify Himself.
   ❏ praise God, because He is up to something more than I can see.

2. Is there a problem for which I blame God? Explain.

3. What disobedience on my part is associated with this problem?

December 15

1. I am able to express myself well about my belief about

   ❏ Jesus as the Son of God.
   ❏ the Bible as the infallible Word of God.
   ❏ salvation.
   ❏ sanctification.
   ❏ other

2. I would like to express myself more clearly about

3. God has used my explanation, when I have shared it with others, in the areas of

4. If I borrow someone else's words, they have no value or power because

5. I will begin today to allow God to pass on His absolute truth through me because

DECEMBER 16

1. The things that hinder my communication with God are

   ❏ mental "woolgathering."
   ❏ my preoccupation with this world.
   ❏ the unseen world.
   ❏ other

2. My wrestling is to be

   ❏ for others.
   ❏ with God.
   ❏ before God with the things of this world.
   ❏ before God because I am more than a conqueror through Him.
   ❏ before God because it makes an impact in His kingdom.

3. Following is a description of my most recent reaction to something unpleasant that God permitted in my life.

DECEMBER 17

1. Matching:

   a. The gospel of God creates the sense of need for
   b. The gospel is hidden to those
   c. Jesus said, "Ask,
   d. Through our asking, God puts His process in motion,
   e. As redemption creates the life of God in us,
   f. The only thing that can possibly satisfy the need is

   ___ it also creates the things which belong to that life.
   ___ and it will be given you."
   ___ who are perishing, whose minds the god of this age has blinded, who do not believe.
   ___ the gospel.
   ___ what created the need.
   ___ creating something in us that was nonexistent until we asked.

2. Sharing my own experience creates no real need in the listener because

3. The last time I spoke life to someone was

DECEMBER 18

1. Do I truly believe God sovereignly controls my circumstances?

2. Am I loyal to the Lord Jesus Christ in every circumstance?

3. A time when circumstances fell apart, bringing the realization that I had been disloyal to Him, was when

4. The results of my faithfulness to God are that

   ❑ He is free to do His work through me.
   ❑ I will do work for God.
   ❑ I will serve Him.
   ❑ I will carry out responsibilities He places on me.
   ❑ I will not complain.
   ❑ I will not expect Him to explain everything.
   ❑ He will be able to use me as He used His own Son.

DECEMBER 19

1. One person I view sympathetically is

2. Am I willing to be the firm one, so that God may be viewed as the tender one? I will do this by

3. Healing and blessing come only after

4. When a person says he or she cannot live up to such a high standard, I will

5. Do I actually believe that the only real peace is that based on a personal relationship with Jesus Christ? Why is this a key point when confronting others?

December 20

1. The death of Jesus Christ on the cross was absolutely essential because

2. I become a traitor to Jesus Christ if I try to help lost people with my sympathy and understanding since

3. If I want to help the lost, I must be in a right relationship with God because

4. Do I know Scripture well enough to apply it "surgically"? If not, am I willing to study until I do?

5. Am I willing to use the Word in a confrontational manner?

December 21

1. Meditate on this.

My Experience	My Redemption
• It does not make redemption real.	• It is reality.
• I go beyond this when I am born again.	• Results in me becoming identified with Jesus Christ.
• If I am left with only this then I am left with something not produced by redemption.	• Experiences produced by this prove themselves by leading me beyond myself.
• It is only of value if it keeps me at my Source of truth, Jesus Christ.	• I see that reality produced the experiences.
• It must never be dearer to me than my Lord.	• I must allow Him to be Lord over me.
• I do not care what I experience.	• I am sure of Him.
• Do not talk of experiences.	• Faith based on God's revealed truth is the only faith there is.

2. I must break the habit of talking about my experience because

December 22

1. Choose the statements that apply to me.

   When God begins to draw me to Himself I

   ❏ react positively to the truth He is revealing.
   ❏ discuss and deliberate as if to decide my response.
   ❏ deliberately commit myself.
   ❏ am willing to act solely on what He says.
   ❏ find that I am grounded on reality as certain as God's throne.

2. Place a check before all true statements.

   In preaching the gospel I know

   ❏ I must focus on the will.
   ❏ there must be a surrender of the will.
   ❏ I must deliberately step out, placing my faith in God and in His truth.
   ❏ my own mental understanding becomes a hindrance.
   ❏ I must ignore and leave my feelings behind.

3. One old way of looking at things I must separate myself from is

December 23

1. My decision about the gospel of Jesus Christ is that

   ❏ I have accepted God's verdict on sin.
   ❏ I have an interest in the death of Jesus.
   ❏ I want to be completely dead to all interest in sin, worldliness, and self.
   ❏ I do not want sin to die in me.
   ❏ at any cost I want to be identified with the death of Jesus.
   ❏ I have already come to know that my old life was crucified with Him.
   ❏ the life of God in me enables me to obey the voice of Jesus Christ.

2. The last time I had a glimpse of what I would be like if it were not for Him, I noticed I was

3. When I was first introduced into God's kingdom I believed God saved me to give me joy, and I now realize

December 24

1. Explain why a life with almighty God is a secure life, in spite of all appearances.

2. It is dangerous and unsure to live without God because

3. My view of walking in the light is that
   - ❏ it is high and wonderful.
   - ❏ I could never live up there.
   - ❏ I can get there through God's grace.
   - ❏ there is plenty of room to live and grow.

December 25

1. Matching with fill-in answers:

   a. Jesus Christ was born _____ this world,

   b. He did _____ out of history;

   c. Jesus Christ is not the best human _____,

   d. He is not _____ becoming God, but God _____,

   e. His life is the _____ and the _____

   f. Our Lord's birth was _____,

   ___ He is a _____ for whom the human race can take no credit at all.

   ___ God coming into human flesh, coming into it from outside.

   ___ entering through the most humble (lowliest) of doors.

   ___ not _____ it.

   ___ the appearance of God in human form.

   ___ He came into history from the _____.

2. Has the Lord come into my life from outside?

3. My life is like a Bethlehem for the Son of God in the following ways:

December 26

1. Explain what sin is and why Jesus had to face it at Calvary.

2. Check statements that apply to you.

   The imparting of His perfection through a full work and deep touch has

   ❏ caused me to know what sin is.
   ❏ worked deep in my unconscious realm.
   ❏ resulted in a profound understanding of sin.

3. To "walk in the light as He is in the light" means that

   ❏ if I don't hold anything back, or try to hide things from God, then this truth will be revealed to me–that I am completely cleansed by Jesus' blood.
   ❏ I know clearly on a conscious level what sin really is.
   ❏ God's love working in me causes me to hate, with the Holy Spirit's hatred for sin, anything not in line with God's holiness.
   ❏ everything of darkness drives me closer to the center of the light.

December 27

1. The last battle of my will I fought in God's presence and won was over

2. The time period involved in this battle was

3. This issue has no hold over me now because

4. The issue or battle of my will that I need to get before the Lord now is over

5. Surrender to God begins for me and others when we

6. As God brings me to a major turning point I become more and more

   ❏ slow, lazy, and useless.
   ❏ expectant, willing, on fire; eager to give my utmost for His highest– my best for His glory.

DECEMBER 28

1. When God brings me into a new situation my focus is on

   ❑ my spiritual life, that is, obeying God.
   ❑ my natural life, that is, my performance before others.

2. What can I do to insure that I will respond in a way more pleasing to God?

3. Some areas where I need conversion from the natural to the spiritual are

4. Am I refusing to convert myself? Explain.

DECEMBER 29

1. If I do not walk in the clear vision of God's will,

   ❑ I will sink into bondage.
   ❑ I will become a slave to ideas and views foreign to my Lord.
   ❑ I may compare myself with others, or judge them.
   ❑ my life could consist in the abundance of things.

2. Do I lie back and bask in the memory of the wonderful experience I had when God revealed His will to me? If so, explain why I have lost the clear vision.

3. A New Testament standard has been revealed to me by the light of God, and

   ❑ I am trying to measure up.
   ❑ I am not inclined to measure up.
   ❑ my conscience does not respond to the truth.
   ❑ I am continuing on in the truth revealed.
   ❑ I have gone back as a deserter.

DECEMBER 30

1. The Lord doesn't patch up my qualities, but completely remakes me because

2. That which God places within me is

   The responsibility I have in this is

3. Two ways God has specifically withered my confidence in my own natural virtues and power is by

4. I am only able to meet Jesus Christ's demand in love, patience, and purity by

DECEMBER 31

1. Am I looking forward with eagerness to all that God has for my future? Explain.

2. As I remember my yesterdays, do anxieties arise within me? Explain.

3. Relate one or two memories of my past sins or blunders God has used for growth in my life or the lives of others.

4. Do these past errors cause me to lean more on my Lord today? Explain.

5. As I enter a new year, I will do so thoughtfully and not impulsively because

Note to the Reader

The publisher invites you to share your response to the message of this book by writing Discovery House Publishers, P. O. Box 3566, Grand Rapids, MI 49501, U.S.A. For information about other Discovery House books and music, contact us at the same address or call 1-800-653-8333.